Secrets to successful

long-term care planning,

caregiving, and

crisis management

Aging
Answers

Valerie VanBooven
RN, BSN, CMC

LTC Expert Publications, LLC • St. Louis, Missouri

First printing 2004

Published by:
LTC EXPERT PUBLICATIONS, LLC
2060 Wealdwood Ct.
St. Louis, MO 63122
877-529-0550
Email: *Valerie@seniorcaresolutionsinc.com*
Web: *http://www.theltcexpert.com*

ISBN 0-9743373-0-7
LCCN 2003094874

ATTENTION CORPORATIONS, UNIVERSITIES, COLLEGES, AND PROFESSIONAL ORGANIZATIONS: Quantity discounts are available on bulk purchases of this book for educational, gift purposes, or as premiums for increasing magazine subscriptions or renewals. Special books or book excerpts can also be created to fit specific needs. For information, please contact LTC Expert Publications, at 877-529-0550, or on the web at *www.theltcexpert.com.*

Cover and Interior Design © TLC Graphics, www.TLCGraphics.com
Edited by JoAnne Lorensen, M.Ed., NCC
Printed and bound by Bang Printing, Brainerd, Minnesota

Dedication

This book is dedicated to adult children of aging parents, care-givers, seniors, and people who are tireless advocates of the elderly, and quality long-term care. There are those of you who no longer have a voice – I am proud to have served as your advocate and your protector in a time of need. For those of you who still have a voice, keep expressing, keep advocating, and keep reaching out and educating others. From you, I learn something new everyday. To my family, friends, and loved ones, thank you for your patience, your support, your encouragement, and your influence. I have started to believe that anything is possible.

Table of Contents

Introduction

Our population is aging at an incredible rate. Today we are living longer, healthier lives. With longevity comes a series of very important decisions that we need to make regarding our health care and our financial situation.

Statistics tell us that there is a significant chance that we will need long-term care at some point in our lives. With that in mind, the following are the questions most frequently asked by baby-boomers, and seniors alike:

- Who will care for me?
- Where will I be cared for?
- How will I pay for my care?
- How can I guarantee that care for my aging parent, or my own care is quality care?
- Where do I find resources to help me locate and afford the best care possible?

There are an overwhelming amount of long-term care services offered for seniors today. Navigating the long-term care maze can be complicated and confusing to say the least. However, this book is designed to provide simple, effective information and resources that can be easily used and implemented in any situation, giving you the *"Aging Answers: Secrets to Successful Long-Term Care Planning, Caregiving, and Crisis Management"*.

Part one of the book discusses planning ahead for long-term care. This includes understanding what long-term care is, the effects that it has on our families and careers, who pays for it, insurance options, asset based planning, and legal issues that need to be addressed.

Part two covers issues related to caring for an aging adult and managing care when it is already needed. Some seniors and their families may already be experiencing a long-term care crisis. Those families need simple and effective information on resources available, definitions, and suggestions that will enable them to know what questions to ask and where to look for help.

Finally, the book includes the "**Aging Answers Rolodex**". This is a list of important agencies and websites that offer further information and resources for planning ahead, as well as for caregiving today.

VALERIE VANBOOVEN RN, BSN, CMC
St. Louis, Missouri
October 2003

Part One

Planning Ahead
For Long-Term Care

The Unimaginable:
A Reality for Two Families

The following **true** stories are illustrations of families who are currently faced with decisions regarding long-term care. They are included here to help you understand what happens to families when they are faced with some overwhelming decisions. Neither of these families did anything in the way of planning ahead financially for long-term care. Both ended up spending most of their assets to pay for the extraordinary costs associated with nursing homes and home care. The **secret** to avoiding financial devastation is to do whatever you can to prepare for the future.

An Early Diagnosis...

Steven and Patricia had been married for 30 years. Steven was 56 years old when he was diagnosed with Alzheimer's disease. The symptoms had been slowly creeping up on him. He had started to forget his way to his clients' homes. These were people he had done business with for 10–15 years. He was a very successful salesman.

One afternoon as he was attempting some household repairs, he hit his head on the bottom of a cabinet in the kitchen and fell to the floor. He was not hurt badly, but after a day or two his neck really began to bother him. His doctor prescribed a cat scan of the neck and head. There was nothing wrong with his neck, just some muscle strain. But something more ominous was showing up on that CAT scan. Plaques and tangles in his brain. These are signs of Alzheimer's disease. Steven and his family were devastated. As Patricia looked back, she could see some of the signs...the forgetfulness, confusion, and difficulty concentrating on tasks. He was not able to read the newspaper without getting frustrated, and even after seeing the eye-doctor, he still couldn't seem to read the paper well. He struggled with directions, and with paperwork that he had been using for years in his business. He became short-tempered and easily frustrated. Patricia thought depression might have been the issue, but she never imagined this.

Steven remained at home with Patricia for several years. She cared for him constantly as the symptoms progressed. He would put on 5 shirts instead of one. Piles of socks littered the bedroom floor...he seemed to be searching for something. Steven appeared to know at times that he was having problems remembering and rationalizing. Other times, he simply did not know what he was doing, or why.

Patricia called me 2 years after Steven's initial diagnosis. She needed a break. She needed to get out of the house and start enjoying life again. She had been a prisoner in her own home for at least a year. She was afraid to leave her husband, even to go to the grocery. Their children were grown and had families of their own. They came by to help but it wasn't enough. Patricia was only 55 years old when I met her. She was a good, loving wife, but angry and disappointed that the best years they could have spent together were taken away.

Patricia hired some in-home caregivers to come to the house 3 days a week for a few hours at a time. She found the break she needed. Steven's health insurance would not pay for this type of care because it was not SKILLED care. It was considered long-term care. He would not recover, he would not get any better, and he would need this type of care for the rest of his life. Steven did not have to be admitted to the hospital for that diagnosis. His body was healthy. Potentially, he could live for 10 or more years.

Patricia and Steven are still privately paying for that care (they had no long-term care insurance). His initial diagnosis was 6 years ago. Steven is now living in a residential facility near their home. Patricia had to return to work to make ends meet. She is now 59 years old. Steven's retirement and all their investments are depleted.

Patricia asked me not too long ago: "Who will pay for MY care, when I need it? There is no private funding left. Who will care for me? Where will I be cared for?"

———————————————————

This story is true, and possibly one of the worst-case scenarios. However, it illustrates that planning ahead for long-term care is not just for people in their 70's and 80's. Long-term care can affect anyone at anytime. Life-style accidents, and diseases like Parkinson's, Multiple Sclerosis (MS), Alzheimer's disease, or strokes, can happen any time.

———————————————————

It Happened So Fast...

An ambulance pulls up to the Emergency Room door around 4a.m., with a 67-year-old male, complaining of right-sided weakness. He was getting up to use the bathroom, and suddenly realized that he was unable to walk, or use his right arm. He managed to wake his wife and tell her that something was wrong. After a few minutes of analyzing the situation, his wife dialed 911.

Robert is rolled into the busy Emergency Room, and assisted onto a gurney in room #4. Nurses and doctors assess the situation, start IV's, and give him some life saving medicine that will stop the progression of the STROKE. His wife, Nancy, is in the waiting room and has now contacted all three of their children. Susan lives the closest, and is on her way. The boys, Tom and Joe, live out of town, and will make flight arrangements in the morning.

After several hours in the ER, a physician working on Robert's case approaches Nancy and Susan. He tells them both that there is good news, and there is bad news. The good news is: Robert is going to make it. He is stable and ready to be transferred upstairs to a regular bed. The bad news: Robert will need therapy and rehabilitative services to hopefully restore the use of his right arm and leg. He will need to learn to walk again, to dress himself, bathe himself, and transfer himself from the bed to a chair.

There is no guarantee as to how long the rehabilitation will take, and no guarantee of full recovery. But with hard work, there is hope.

THE RECOVERY PROCESS

Robert spends three nights in the hospital. Physical therapy and occupational therapy had been implemented immediately. At the beginning of day four, Robert is transferred to the local nursing home for skilled care and rehabilitation under Medicare. As long as Robert makes progress with his therapy, Medicare will pay for his care and room and board at the nursing home for up to 100 days.

Nancy is by his side every day, encouraging Robert to improve, celebrating every step that he is now making with the assistance of a walker. Susan visits regularly. The boys have already come and gone, but call daily for updates and to send their love.

Words No One Wants to Hear

Three weeks into Robert's rehabilitation, a care-planning meeting is held, and Nancy is invited to attend. In a cramped conference room, doctors, nurses, and therapists sit around a large table. Nancy is informed that Robert has hit a plateau. This means that although he has made good progress over the last few weeks, he has now hit a point where he is making little to no further progress. He can walk with a walker, but will need assistance with bathing and dressing, and some assistance transferring from the bed to a chair.

That's it?

By Medicare rules and regulations, Robert no longer qualifies for skilled care. Nancy is provided with various options. Robert can go home, and potentially receive some home health care as long as he is deemed "homebound". That home health care will consist of a 45-minute visit by a physical therapist and occupational therapist on alternating days. This type of home care is brief, and will probably not last much longer than a couple of weeks. It does not include and assistance with Robert's daily living needs, like bathing, dressing, and eating.

At the end of the week Robert is discharged from the nursing home and returns home with his wife, and his daughter Susan, to take care of him.

Susan is 35 years old. She has 3 children of her own and works full time. Her children are busy preteens and teenagers, who are involved in soccer, cheerleading, and basketball. Susan's husband also works full time.

Susan knows that her mother, Nancy, will be able to primarily care for her father, but will need some help. How much help is the question...

HOME FRONT

Robert is happy to be in his own bed, in his own home, with his wife. He has made enough progress to get himself up from the bed and into a wheelchair with minimal assistance. He can walk through the house with the aid of a walker. He cannot fully dress himself, or bathe without assistance.

Nancy spends her mornings helping Robert prepare for the day. She carefully helps him shower, dress, shave, and helps him to the bathroom.

Susan made it a point to visit daily for a couple of weeks after the homecoming. She now visits 2-3 times per week, allowing her mother to get out of the house and do a little shopping or run errands.

Nancy has decided to hire a nurse's aid to come to the house 3 days a week so that she can get some much needed rest and assistance with running the household.

Medicare does not pay for these services, so Robert and Nancy will be paying $16.50 per hour, for 5 hours of care per day, 3 days per week, which equals about $990.00 per month, or close to $12,000/ year for in-home care.

This extra $990.00 per month is not something they had factored in to their expenses upon retirement. **How many of us can easily afford to factor in the equivalent of a house payment on a monthly basis, so unexpectedly?**

CHANGES

Robert was stable for quite some time. A few months after returning home, he began feeling weak and not so well. Robert was diagnosed with pneumonia. As he became progressively weaker, Nancy found it impossible to get him out of bed without assistance.

Robert was once again admitted to the hospital for a round of IV antibiotics, and then discharged after two days to his home, and to the care of his family.

Robert and Nancy increased the in-home care to 5 hours per day, 5 days per week, with assistance from Susan on the weekends.

Their out of pocket expenses were now reaching a level close to $20,000 per year for in-home care.

Robert would live at home for another two years, with the assistance of his wife, daughter, and in-home care.

More Changes, More Cost

As time progressed, Robert became increasingly confused and forgetful. Nancy cared for him a long as she could, but there came a time when Robert was requiring 24 hour a day care and assistance. She was no longer able to keep him at home.

After careful consideration, and with the help of her children, Nancy placed Robert in a local nursing home. The cost per day for a semi-private room was $140. That adds up to $4200 per month, or $50,400 per year.

Nancy also had to add in the extra expenses of supplies and medications. These costs totaled about $840 per month, or $10,080 per year (about 20% over the cost of room and board).

The total bill for Robert's care had now jumped from around $20,000 per year to $60,480 per year!

Within two years Robert and Nancy's entire life savings and retirement nest egg was gone.

Next Steps

Although not all nursing homes have Medicaid beds, this one had a few available. Robert was immediately put on the waiting list. Robert was on the waiting list for two years. When Robert and Nancy's money ran out two years later, he was allowed to stay in the same bed, but was now Medicaid eligible.

At that point, the federal and state government paid for Robert's care.

Nancy was left with only the home and a car, as well as her Social Security Income. The rainy day money they had set aside was now completely gone, along with any inheritance they had hoped to pass on to their children.

Conclusion

Robert and Nancy's situation was financially devastating. Obviously they had not planned ahead. Long-term care insurance would have paid for the home health aid and most of the nursing home costs associated with Robert's care. Robert would have been able to stay at home a little longer with the appropriate resources and financial assistance. Nancy would have been left with enough money to live comfortably and with peace of mind. Although long-term care insurance cannot take away the emotional pain of a family dealing with a chronically ill parent or spouse, it can alleviate the financial burden and provide security by preserving the family's assets.

Secret #1:
Most of Us Don't Understand What Long-Term Care Really Means!

The first step to successful long-term care planning is:
Understanding what long-term care is,
and how it effects all of us.

L ong-term care IS so many things. It affects so many people. Navigating through the long-term care maze has been the best-kept secret in America. However, as our population ages, we are "letting the cat out of the bag" so to speak. Long-term care means needing care for a long period of time. Greater than 90 days. A hospitalization for pneumonia, or heart surgery, or kidney stones, is not considered long-term care. A diagnosis of Parkinson's Disease, Alzheimer's Disease, Emphysema, a stroke, Lou Gehrig's Disease, or Chronic Obstructive Pulmonary Disease (COPD), (just to name a few), ARE diseases and conditions that at some point may require long-term care. Some of the conditions mentioned are manageable, but not curable. We can manage the symptoms of, and possibly slow the progression of Alzheimer's disease, but we cannot cure it (yet). Long-term care does NOT always mean that we are bound for the nursing home. In fact, 80% of long-term care is being provided in a home-like setting.

Only 20% is being provided in a nursing home. This chapter is devoted to explaining why we need long-term care, who needs long-term care, and the different ways people are affected by it.

Longevity

A long life. We like to hear those words, and rightfully so! Everyone wants a long happy life. We strive for that. Being healthy and financially comfortable throughout our lives is a blessing. Since 1900, medical science has extended the average life expectancy by 31 years. In 2001, the CDC tells us that the average life expectancy for a woman is 79.8 years, and for a man about 74.4 years. Deaths from heart disease, cancer, and stroke are down. It is projected that more than 1 million centenarians (people age 100 and over) will be living in the United States by the middle of this century, but only about 15% of those seniors will be able to live completely independently.

So what do all the statistics really mean for us in our day-to-day lives? It means that we have a lot to look forward to. It means that we will be able to enjoy our families and our grandchildren for a longer period of time. My own great-grandmother lived to be 101.5 years old. And yes, she made it on the "Today Show" with Willard Scott, with her picture on the side of a jar of Smucker's Jelly.

But how did she live out the last 5 years of her life? In a nursing home, with a roommate. It was not a terrible situation. She was well cared for, but in a nursing home all the same.

Being 100 and Mowing the Grass

How many 100 year-olds can actually mow the grass in their yards? How many of them are currently able to get in the car and safely drive to the grocery store, pick up a few things, and drive back home? How about seeing well enough to balance a checkbook, or being strong enough to do a couple of loads of laundry? Surely there are many. We hear about them all the time. We ask them what their secret to a long healthy life really is…. and their response? "I drank a glass of wine every evening, and never washed my face with soap."

There is really no guaranteed predictor of longevity, and less guarantee of healthy, uncomplicated longevity. There is a 50% chance that if we reach age 65, we will need some form of long-term care (assistance with activities of daily living), at some point in our lives. Those are incredibly high odds.

Longevity means a higher population of frail elderly who will need assistance with bathing, dressing, toileting, transferring, eating, and continence. These are all basic activities of daily living (ADLs).

So, will you die peacefully in your sleep? That's the goal, right? But what if it doesn't exactly happen that way... What if there are a few bumps in the road along the way? Chances are that with the medical technology we have today, we might recover from a major illness, fully or partially. There is no crystal ball, or magic way to tell just how long we might live, or if we will be in good health.

The best thing we can do for ourselves, and for our families, is to take an active role in planning ahead. The information in this book is designed to simplify that planning process, and help make it less stressful.

54 Million Caregivers in Our Country Today

A recent study by the National Family Caregivers Association, tells us that 54 million families are caring for an aging parent or family member in some regard. That equals about one in four families. That study also suggests that 54% of the caregivers are female.

Long-Term Care is a Woman's Issue

Nancy married a man 10 years her senior. At age 67 Robert had a stroke that left him with right-sided paralysis. He suddenly needed 24 hour care. He was not able to bath, or dress himself. He could not transfer from a bed to a chair. Nancy became an instant caregiver. Their daughter Susan was 35 years old when her father had his stroke. She could see that her mother needed more help at home. Susan had her own family, and career. She made the choice to pass up the next promotion and work part-time, so that she could help her parents at home, and take care of her own family as well.

Long-term care is a family issue, but it is more often a woman's issue. Throughout history women have been the caregivers in our lives. As we have seen, women also live longer than men on average. From beginning to end, women often care for family members young and old. Now as our population begins to age, it is even more important that we understand what lies before us.

Although we see increases in male caregivers all the time, the fact remains, that when it comes to Long-term care for our family members and our spouses, today women carry the weight.

Daughters, daughters-in-law, wives, sisters, and nieces often accept the role of caregiver for aging adults in the family. Across the U.S. there are women commonly referred to as "the sandwich generation", who are playing dual roles in their families. They are often a mother themselves, but caring for their own aging parents at the same time. The level of stress and frustration can be over-whelming. Careers are being put on hold, and promotions passed up, in order to accommodate the busy schedules of their children, and their parents. Even so, there is still not enough time for these women to meet everyone's needs. A financial burden results as well.

Women in America also tend to marry men who are older than them. Therefore, they often end up caring for their chronically ill spouse in later years. When this happens, it is sometimes the case that all of the retirement funding and assets are used by the "ill" spouse for long-term care, leaving nothing in savings to care for the "well" spouse later in life.

It is estimated that one out of two women will need long-term care at some point in their lives. One out of three men will also require long-term care. So why do more women need services? Our life expectancy is still longer than the average male.

Long-Term Care Is a Family Issue

THE WALTON'S NO LONGER EXIST!

Nancy and Robert had three children. Susan, Tom, and Joe. All of the children were adults with careers and families. Susan was the only child living within 100 miles of her parents. The others had been transferred to distant cities, or had moved on for better opportunity. Susan was Nancy's only consistent source of help.

The Walton Family lived in a large home on the family farm (Walton's Mountain). Parents, grandparents, and children all lived under one roof. If grandmother or grandfather needed assistance, several people were available to help at any time. We don't live like that much anymore. Families are in transition. Adult children are transferred to other cities to work, or they leave small towns for more opportunity in larger cities. Most seniors today have one or more children who live at least an hour away, if not clear across the country.

If an aging family member needs help, it may be up to the children to decide who moves back home, or who brings Mom or Dad to live with them in another city.

Families are smaller. Our population is aging, because we are living longer and having fewer children. Therefore, the ratio of workers to retirees is shrinking, and the number of caregivers is too.

Long-Term Care Is a Workplace Issue

EFFECTS ON THE WORKPLACE

Susan worked for a large computer company in her city. She was well on her way to a big promotion, one that she was looking forward to. She tried to manage her own family and her parents' needs as a full-time worker for about 6 months. She soon realized that something had to give. The stress was over-whelming. Her children needed her, her husband needed her, and her parents were in crisis. She passed on the promotion, and started working part-time to satisfy all of those needs.

In 1997, The National Alliance for Caregiving and AARP conducted a study that revealed some startling statistics. The study concluded that two-thirds of caregivers work either full or part-time. Over half of those caregivers reported that they had to make some sort of workplace adjustments in order to continue caring for their aging family member. Most of those adjustments included coming in late, leaving early, taking a leave of absence, working less hours, turning down promotions, taking early retirement, or giving up work completely, all of which impact the employer as well as the employee.

In that same year, Metropolitan Life Insurance Company did a study revealing that these adjustments were costing employers between $11.4 and $29 billion dollars per year in lost productivity. In 1999, MetLife studied the cost of caregiving in lost wages, pensions, and Social Security benefits, which showed that for an individual caregiver, the cost on average to be $656,000.

Secret #2:
There is a Common Misconception That We Are Already Covered for Long-Term Expenses

The second step to successful long-term care planning is:
Understanding that your current health insurance
was never designed to pay for long-term care.

"I'm Already Covered, Right?"

There is a common misconception that health insurance will pay for the cost of long-term care. Health insurance including Medicare, Medicare Supplements, HMOs, private insurance through employers, and disability insurance were *never* designed to pay for the cost of long-term care. Who is paying for long-term care? 26% of long-term care costs are being paid for out of our own pockets: our savings, retirement income, assets, CD's, stocks, bonds, etc. 44% of long-term care costs are being paid for by a program called Medicaid (not to be confused with Medicare). The other 30% of long-term care costs are paid for by various forms of insurance and government programs.

Medicare and Other Health Insurances

Medicare is a federal health insurance program for people 65 and older, certain people with disabilities, and ESRD (End Stage Renal Disease). It pays for much of your health care, but not all of it. There are some costs you will have to pay yourself.

There are other kinds of health insurance that may help pay the costs that Medicare does not. Medicare Supplements (Medigap Policies) and Long-Term Care Insurance will pick up some of the costs that Medicare will not pay for.

Medicare was implemented in 1965. How many times has Medicare been over-hauled since 1965? NEVER. It was not designed to pay for care related to disease processes such as Alzheimer's disease, Parkinson's, or MS. The average life expectancy was much lower in 1965 because medical technology was not as advanced. Medicare was designed for SHORT-TERM acute care, and short-term rehabilitative stays in a rehab or long-term care facility.

WHAT WILL MEDICARE PAY?

Medicare comes in two parts. Medicare Part A and Part B.

MEDICARE PART A IS HOSPITAL INSURANCE.

Part A pays for inpatient hospital care, **some** skilled nursing facility care, hospice care, and **some** home health care. Most people get Medicare Part A automatically when they turn 65. There is no premium or monthly payment for Part A.

MEDICARE PART B IS MEDICAL INSURANCE.

Part B pays for doctor's services, outpatient hospital care, and some other medical services that Part A doesn't pay for. Part B pays for these services and supplies when they are medically necessary. Part B has a premium that is currently $58.70 per month. Rates change every year.

WHAT WILL MEDICARE A AND B NOT PAY FOR?

Medicare carries some high deductibles. For instance, during a hospital stay, you will automatically have an $840 deductible for days 1-60. On day 61, you are responsible for $210 (your deductible) per day through day 90. On day 91, you pay $420 per day (your deductible) through day 150. This amounts to a substantial out-of-pocket expense for the Medicare recipient.

For a skilled nursing facility stay, Medicare pays for days 1-20. On day 21 you pay $105.00 per day deductible through day 100.

Also, you will be responsible for 20% for most covered services under Part B, 50% for outpatient mental health treatment, and a co-pay for outpatient hospital services.

Medicare was never designed to pay for **long-term care.** In other words, if you will be living in a nursing home, or if you will need around the clock care at home, Medicare does not pay for these services. Medicare is for acute medical care, and rehabilitative care only, otherwise called *skilled care.*

Defining Skilled Care vs. Custodial Care

Skilled care is defined as care that is prescribed by a physician, and performed by a licensed health care professional, like a nurse, physical therapist, or occupational therapist. Some examples of skilled care include: some wound care, IV antibiotics, or physical therapy immediately after a stroke. **Custodial care** is another term for private pay care. This type of care can be performed by home health aids, or other unlicensed caregivers, like family members. Some examples of custodial care include bathing, dressing, transferring from the bed to a chair, or toileting.

A Medicare Supplement or Medigap policy will only cover some or all of the deductibles described above. This is a policy that you will have to purchase separately. Medicare supplements will **not** pay for (custodial) long-term care costs. They simply cover the deductibles under Medicare and sometimes pay for a few extras.

Long-Term Care Insurance will not cover Medicare deductibles like a Medigap policy will, but long-term care insurance will pay for all of the costs associated with long-term (custodial) nursing home care, in-home care, assisted living, and adult day care.

Medicare Supplements

Medicare Supplements, often referred to as Medigap plans, are purchased through private insurance companies to help fill the "gaps" that Medicare leaves behind. Medicare Supplements pick up the co-pays and deductibles associated with standard Medicare. There are ten standardized plans available labeled "A" through "J". Each plan has a different set of benefits. Medicare Supplements also do not cover the cost of long-term care; they simply pay deductibles and co-pays that Medicare does not.

HMOs

HMOs are Health Maintenance Organizations. An HMO will require that the participant use certain doctors and hospital systems in their area. HMOs are also for short acute care stays in hospitals, and for short rehabilitative stays in skilled nursing facilities. They do not pay for the cost of long-term care.

Private Insurance

Private health insurance through an employer, or previous employer is essentially the same as HMOs, as far as coverage. Standard health insurance, no matter how great the benefit, will ultimately not cover long-term care.

Disability Insurance

Disability insurance covers household expenses, and is designed as income replacement. It will pay for things like groceries, rent, and utilities. This insurance was not designed to cover the added expense of long-term care.

Veteran's Administration Benefits

Many Veterans mistakenly believe that when they need long-term care, their VA benefits will pay the expense. VA benefits for long-term care are available, but the majority of those benefits are reserved for people with service connected disabilities. Check with your local VA office for more information.

Secret #3:
Relying on Government Assistance is a NOT a Good Planning Strategy

The third step in successful long-term care planning is:
Understanding that relying on Medicaid (the government)
to pay for your long-term care expenses is not a good idea,
and should be avoided if at all possible.

Medicaid Defined

Medicaid was established by federal law (Title XIX of the Social Security Act), and is administered by each state individually. Medicaid is a program for poor or "impoverished" people, and people with high medical costs. Congress established Medicaid to provide a "safety net" for people who had no other way to pay for their health care or long-term care.

Medicaid is the long-term care payer of last resort for the frail elderly, persons with mental retardation, and those with physical or developmental disabilities.

Most long-term care and services such as prescription drugs, eyeglasses, and dental care are provided at each state's discretion.

When money is scarce, these services may be the most vulnerable, not because of ill will on the part of the state decision makers, but because there may be nowhere else to cut state budgets.

Medicaid is a highly flawed program. States continue to make decisions about Medicaid that among other things, will effect the amount of long-term care assistance available in each state, the eligibility criteria and number of persons eligible for that assistance, and the types of services that will be reimbursed.

"Income Cap" States vs. "Medically Needy" States

A state may provide long-term care services in nursing facilities or private community settings to persons whose gross income (without deductions) falls under an "income cap" set by the states. The income cap is generally set at 3 times the Social Security Income standard (currently $1,635). The eligible person must report the income he or she has to pay for the cost of nursing home care, and the state will pay the balance of the cost.

The income cap is absolute. A person whose income is $1 above the cutoff cannot get any assistance from Medicaid even though they have no other way to pay for care. This is commonly known as the "Medicaid Gap", and no spend down of income is allowed.

Income cap states include:

Alabama	Alaska	Arkansas
Colorado	Delaware	Florida
Idaho	Louisiana	Mississippi
Nevada	New Mexico	Oklahoma
Oregon	South Carolina	South Dakota
Texas	Wyoming	

The rest of the states are described as "medically needy" states. In a "medically needy" state, a person who has too much income to qualify for Medicaid services, but has high medical or long-term care bills, can "spend down" their assets in order to qualify. Medicaid "spend down" means that an individual or couple must pay for their own care until their assets have been spent down to meet the asset limitations. Their Social Security Income will go directly to the nursing facility to pay bills, and Medicaid will pick up the rest. In most "medically needy" states, an individual can have no more than $999.99- $2000.00 in assets.

Assets that must be spent down in order to qualify include:

- Cash
- Checking/ saving accounts
- C.D.s
- Savings bonds
- Investment accounts/mutual funds/ stocks
- IRA's and other retirement accounts
- Vacation homes and investment properties
- Second car
- Certain real estate or personal property not in use.

Assets that a person can keep include:

- A home, (a principal residence)
- Household goods
- Personal effects
- Automobile – one per household
- Life insurance (no more than $1500 in cash surrender value)
- Prepaid burial plan and space or designated life insurance policy up to $1500.00
- Property essential to the individual's self support (perhaps a small business).
- Income producing property – other than cash, with some restrictions (like farmed land).

Prenuptial Agreements

This is a second marriage. "What's mine is mine, what's his is his. They won't touch MY money for HIS long-term care, right?"

Yes, they will. Prenuptial agreements hold no weight when it comes to Medicaid. When two people are married, their assets become marital property. So even if Nancy has $1 million dollars, and Robert has $5,000 dollars, is doesn't really matter. They will have to go through the spend down process considering both of their combined assets.

Estate Recovery

With the changes in federal law enacted in August 1993, the state **must** seek recovery of Medicaid expenditures from the estate of a deceased individual who was 55 or older when he or she received assistance. This means that when the person on Medicaid dies, the state will collect the amount they spent on that person's care from the remaining estate. The state must include all real estate and personal property and other assets included within an estate under the state's probate law. The state may include other property in which the individual had an interest at the time of death. If the deceased Medicaid recipient has a spouse still living in the home (community spouse), that spouse can usually continue living in the home until his or her death, before the state will seek recovery.

Transferring Assets – "I'll just give it all away!"

When a person applies for Medicaid to pay for long-term care, federal law requires the state to consider recent transfers of assets and monetary gifts. If a person or his or her spouse has transferred assets for less than fair market value in the 36 months (3 years) prior to applying for Medicaid, or at any time after applying, the applicant will be considered "ineligible" for a period of time based on the amount transferred. In the case of assets transferred to a "trust" the **look back period** is 60 months. The look back period means that the state can go back 5 years and see if any transfers have been made and add them (based on a specific calculation) to the ineligibility period.

Divorce

If Robert and Nancy had given $120,000 to their wonderful daughter Susan, for safe keeping 4 years prior to Robert's stroke, Robert would almost immediately be eligible for Medicaid.

But what if Susan's husband Scott decided that he wanted a divorce? Technically, in most states that money would be considered marital property, and would be divided in half, leaving Susan with only $60,000 of her parent's money.

Lawsuits

Susan has her parent's $120,000 in a bank account in her name. Husband Scott is in a car accident, and the other party sues Scott for damages beyond what his insurance company will pay. The plaintiff's lawyer sees $120,000 sitting in their account. If he wins the case, they may lose it all.

Financial Aid for College

Susan and Scott have a daughter who will be 18 in a few months. She is looking forward to going away to college. The family applies for financial aid, but because they have Susan's parent's $120,000 in their account, their daughter does not qualify for financial aid.

Buying Toys

Susan and Scott have always been fairly responsible, but have decided that they need that new boat. Robert and Nancy won't know if they borrow just $20,000. They will be sure to pay it back…. Eventually.

Secret #4:
Planning Ahead for
Long-Term Care Means
Evaluating All of the Options

The fourth step to successful long-term care planning is:
Understanding what Long-Term Care Insurance is,
and the different types of long-term care insurance
available on the market today.

Traditional Long-Term Care Insurance

Traditional Long-Term Care Insurance used to be viewed as "nursing home insurance" because most policies from 15 years ago only offered that one option. Today, that is hardly the case. Long-Term Care Insurance now covers adult day care, in-home care, assisted living, and nursing home care. These policies are considered comprehensive in nature.

WHO CAN'T GET LONG-TERM CARE INSURANCE?

Underwriting Explained

When you apply for a Long-Term Care Insurance plan, you must go through underwriting. Underwriting means that the company will check your medical records to determine what medical problems you may currently have, or have had in the past. They want to know your overall health history. If you have been diagnosed with short-term memory loss, Alzheimer's disease, Parkinson's disease, Multiple Sclerosis, Lou Gehrig's disease, or if you have had a stroke with permanent physical impairment, you may not qualify. People who have survived cancer and are treatment free for a certain length of time can often qualify. Each insurance company has their own underwriting guidelines. It is best to talk to your agent, or call the company directly with any specific questions about health issues. Height and weight are also a consideration when applying. Sometimes the insurance company will send a registered nurse to the home to ask a few questions, and take some more medical history, or they may just call on the phone for a brief interview.

QUALIFYING TO USE THE BENEFITS OF A LONG-TERM CARE INSURANCE PLAN

Activities of Daily Living

When it's time to use your tax qualified Long-Term Care Insurance plan (taxes to be discussed in a later chapter), the insured person must need help or substantial assistance with 2 out of 6 activities of daily living for a period of 90 days or greater. This need for care must be certified by a licensed healthcare practitioner such as a nurse or physician.

These activities of daily living include:

- Bathing
- Dressing
- Eating
- Toileting
- Continence
- Transferring (i.e.moving from the bed to a chair)

Or, the insured must have a cognitive impairment, like Alzheimer's disease or dementia. A cognitive impairment means that although a person may be physically able to perform all of the activities listed above, they cannot remember or rationalize how to do those activities. One example would be bathing. Sometimes people with dementia are physically able to take a bath, but can't remember to do so, or can't remember why this is important. Or, perhaps when getting dressed, they put on 5 shirts instead of one.

Comprehensive vs. Facility Only Plans

COMPREHENSIVE PLANS

A comprehensive plan covers all aspects of long-term care: in-home care, adult day care, assisted living, and nursing home care. These plans are designed to help people stay at home longer, and also assist them with transitions to other levels of care as needed. Most consumers want to stay at home for as long as possible. A comprehensive plan will satisfy that desire.

FACILITY ONLY COVERAGE

Facility only plans are still available on the market today. Facility only plans pay for just that, facility care only. Usually this includes assisted living and nursing home care. A facility only plan makes the most sense for folks who do not have a large network of family and friends around them, and for people who know that this may be their only option in the future. Facility only plans are less costly than comprehensive plans, but again, offer payment only for nursing home and assisted living care. The insured person cannot live at home and use the benefits of a facility only plan.

BENEFIT PERIOD

The benefit period is the length of time the policy will actually pay for care. There are many different benefit periods available including 2 years, 3 years, 4 years, 5 years, 7 years, 10 years, and unlimited lifetime coverage. When purchasing long-term care insurance, keep in mind that premiums are paid for potentially the next 20 years (or until the policy holder needs care), but the plan will only last about as long as the benefit period originally selected.

People often ask, "How do I know which benefit period to choose?" "How do I know how long I might need care?"

Obviously, there is no way to really determine how long a person might need care. However, the best advice is for each individual to take a look at their own personal health history, and their family history. If there is a history of chronic disease such as Alzheimer's, Parkinson's, MS, or Lou Gehrig's disease, it might be worthwhile to consider a longer benefit period.

The average length of stay in a nursing home is about 2.8 years; the average care giving time at home is about 4.1 years.

DAILY BENEFIT AMOUNT

The daily benefit amount is the maximum amount a plan will pay on a daily or weekly basis. Some policies now pay based on a weekly or monthly maximum. In this case, it is important to know the average cost of care in the local area. In the Midwest, for example, the average cost of care for a semi-private nursing home bed is about $135 per day. Therefore, the plan should pay a maximum of $4,050 per month. Currently in New York, the cost of a semi-private nursing home bed is around $250 per day or $7,500 per month. Consider the cost of care in the area where you live, and the cost of care in an area where you might retire, and plan accordingly.

A semi-private room in a nursing home means that two people share a room. A private room in a nursing home means that the room is for one person only. A private room will cost significantly more than a semi-private room. Be sure to factor in the extra cost if a private room is expected.

For some people, the insurance policy's daily benefit amount doesn't need to cover the entire cost of care. If there is some Social Security income, or pension income that can pick up a portion of the long-term care costs, then perhaps some premium can be saved by having a lower daily benefit amount.

Keep in mind, however, that $135/day covers the cost of room and board only in the Midwest, not the added cost of prescription drugs, and supplies such as adult incontinence protection, and other necessities. The additional expense of these items can add as much as 20% on to the cost of a nursing home bed per day.

ELIMINATION PERIOD

The elimination period is similar to a deductible or a waiting period. This is the length of time a person must wait before their plan will begin to pay. Elimination periods vary from company to company, and plan to plan. The elimination period choices include 0 days, 30 days, 60 days, 90 days, 100 days, and 180 days. Some plans will offer to waive the elimination period for home care under certain circumstances, and some offer riders that will eliminate or decrease waiting periods. Be aware that some elimination periods are based on dates of service. Therefore, if only one day of home care is needed per week, and the elimination period is 30 days, it could take as much as 30 weeks to satisfy that elimination period. On the other hand, many companies today will allow one day of home care to count as 7 days toward the elimination period. This is a nice strategy and is useful in encouraging people to stay home longer.

The shorter the elimination period, the more expensive the premium.

INFLATION PROTECTION OPTIONS

The average cost of health care rises anywhere from 4%-7% per year. Therefore, $135 per day today won't be enough coverage 10 years from now when the cost is actually around $250 per day. So it is important to build in some protection against the cost of inflation.

There are typically three types of inflation protection that are available. One is compound inflation protection, which provides an automatic increase in benefits every year (usually at 5%) with no corresponding increase in premium. This is the most expensive inflation protection, but well worth the investment. For consumers who buy long-term care insurance at younger ages, for example anyone under age 70, compound inflation protection offers the most complete coverage.

Simple inflation protection is also usually at 5% per year, but is not compounded. This inflation protection will grow at a slower rate than compound inflation protection, and is often recommended for folks over age 70. There is no corresponding increase in premium.

Finally, there is a future purchase option offered on some plans. This option allows the consumer to decide at a later time whether they would like to by more daily benefit amount to catch up with the current cost of care. If no extra benefit is purchased, the daily benefit amount remains the same, and the premium does not increase. If extra benefit is purchased, the premium increases to the new benefit level. No further underwriting is required for future purchase option benefit increases.

CARE COORDINATION BENEFITS

Some plans will offer care coordination as a built in benefit. Care coordination is a valuable service for both the person receiving care, and for the other family members involved. Long-term care insurers recognize that sometimes it is difficult for a senior or a family member to know which services in their local area might be most appropriate, and give the best quality care available. Care coordinators are licensed professionals such as Registered Nurses and Licensed Social Workers who have experience in home health and coordinating care for seniors in their local areas. Some companies will require the plan member to use a care coordinator designated by the insurer. Other companies will allow a family to choose that care coordinator. They will allot a certain amount of money to be used toward a comprehensive in-home evaluation, and plan of care. Either way, this service is invaluable, and takes the fear and confusion out of selecting a long-term care provider. Care coordinators are not "gatekeepers". They are simply health-care professionals who know the system, and the local resources. They are there for guidance and assistance along the way.

HOME CARE AND COMMUNITY CARE BENEFITS

Home and Community Care includes services provided by a licensed home health agency. This can include services from a Registered Nurse, Licensed Practical Nurse, Physical Therapist, Occupational Therapist, Nurse's Aide, homemaker services (non-medical services), at-home hospice care, and adult day care. Some plans with enhanced home care provisions, or riders, will also allow (with authorization) a friend or family member to provide care. That family member will be reimbursed for their time and expense. Usually, a family member cannot be someone who normally lives in the same home as the person going on claim. In other words, most long-term care insurance companies do not want to pay a spouse to be the sole caregiver.

FACILITY CARE

Facility care most often refers to care received in a Nursing Home, Hospice Facility, or Assisted Living Facility. The plan will usually cover room and board, and nursing care, maintenance or personal care, and hospice care in that facility. Most plans will also offer a bed reservation benefit, meaning that if a person leaves the facility for the weekend, or is hospitalized, the insurer will pay for that amount of time to hold the bed even though the insured is not in the facility. Most bed reservation benefits last about 30 days per policy year.

RESPITE CARE BENEFITS

Respite Care, simply defined, is a break for the caregiver. For example, if daughter Susan is caring for her father, she may need a break form time to time. If she decides to take a long weekend and go on vacation, a formal caregiver can be hired to take her place. Respite care can be received in a nursing home, adult day care, in-home, or in a hospice facility. The insurer will pay the maximum daily benefit, for up to 21 days per year on average. The insured does not have to meet the elimination period in order to use Respite Care benefits.

ALTERNATE PLAN OF CARE

Alternate plan of care usually refers to services that are not already clearly defined in the plan. Most alternate plans of care must be approved by the insurer, but would include services designed to enhance quality of life, or designed to keep a person safe in their home for a longer period of time. One example would be a Personal Emergency Service, like LifeLine, or perhaps a wheelchair ramp that would enhance accessibility to the insured's home.

CAREGIVER TRAINING

Caregiver Training is useful when an informal caregiver needs to learn how to bathe, transfer, feed, or dress someone receiving long-term care. A licensed or formally trained professional will provide the training to the informal caregiver. This ensures that the care being received is quality care, and is provided in a safe and efficient manner. This training will be paid for by the plan.

BELLS AND WHISTLES (THE RIDERS)

Riders can be purchased in addition to the standard long-term care insurance plan, and offer flexibility in plan design.

Shared Benefits

Some plans will allow spouses and families to share benefits. One example would be sharing a benefit between husband and wife. Therefore, husband and wife choose an 8-year plan. If he needs to use 6 years of the plan, she will have 2 years left to use when she needs long-term care. A shared benefit plan might be recommended to a couple who have been married for many years, and who are roughly the same age.

Survivorship

Survivorship typically means that if both spouses are insured by the same company, no claim has been made in 7-10 years, and one spouse passes away, the other spouse's plan will be paid up in full, and there will be no further premium due for the surviving spouse, and coverage will continue.

Return of Premium

Return of premium takes away the fear: "If I don't use it, I will lose it!" This simply means that if a claim has never been made, and the insured person passes away, the premium paid will be returned to the surviving heirs. There are several variations on the theme, and each company handles return of premium differently. Pay close attention to contract language.

Waiver of Premium

In many cases, waiver of premium is a built in feature of a long-term care insurance plan, but in some cases it can be purchased as an extra rider. Waiver of premium means that when the insured goes on claim, and begins using their benefits, they no longer pay premiums to the insurance company. Usually, waiver of premium goes into effect after the elimination period has been satisfied.

Indemnity Plans

The typical long-term care insurance plan is a reimbursement plan, meaning that the insurance company reimburses the care providers after a claim has been sent in. However, some plans now offer an indemnity situation. This type of plan will pay the insured the daily or monthly benefit, and it is up to the insured to pay the care providers. This type of plan is more flexible, and usually more expensive. However, the insured has more options when choosing a care provider. For instance, instead of using a local home health agency, the insured person may want to pay a son or daughter to care for them. Indemnity plans require that the insured, or their legal representative makes good choices about care and is able to use the money wisely.

Important Consideration When Choosing a Long-Term Care Plan

RATINGS

Financial ratings of a company are important when considering purchasing a long-term care insurance plan. The recommendation is to choose a company with an AM BEST rating of A+ or better.

ASSETS

Assets of the insurance company should be in the BILLIONS.

DISCOUNTS

Some long-term care insurers will allow for group discounts through employers, or "affinity" group discounts through a local organization. Senior clubs and organizations all across America offer discounts from 5%-10% on long-term care insurance. Not all companies permit these types of discounts; however there are some discounts that almost all long-term care insurers include in their plans. Those include spousal (or partner) discounts and good health discounts. Spousal discounts are applied when a couple applies for the insurance together. Discounts of this kind range anywhere from 30-50%. Good health discounts are given when the applicant is in excellent health. Each company has it's own underwriting guidelines for health discounts. These will range from 10%-15%.

Tax Considerations

Currently, there are some tax advantages regarding tax qualified long-term care insurance plans. At the Federal level, premium for long-term care insurance falls into the "medical expense" category. So, if the premium (or the premium plus other medical expenses) is over 7.5% of the adjusted gross income, part of that premium is tax deductible. Below is a table that determines how much of that premium is deductible. It is important to talk to a tax advisor or accountant for that information, as it changes every year.

> 40 and younger = $250
> 41 – 50 = $470
> 51 – 60 = $940
> 61 - 70 = $2,510
> 71 and older = $3,130

On the state level, 26 states offer some form of deduction or tax credit for long-term care insurance premiums. In the state of Missouri, for example, premiums are 50% tax deductible. This is an "above the line" deduction, so there is no need to itemize to take advantage of the savings. In Kentucky, the premium is 100% tax deductible. Again, it is important to see an accountant or tax advisor for tax advantages state by state.

TAX QUALIFIED PLANS VS. NON-TAX QUALIFIED PLANS

To make matters a little more complicated, there are two types of standard Long-Term Care Insurance plans available. Tax qualified plans follow the Federal HIPAA law (Health Insurance Portability and Accountability Act). For these plans, the insured must need assistance or help with 2 out of 6 activities of daily living, for a period of 90 days or greater, in order to qualify to use their benefits. This law protects consumers in several ways. It insures that long-term care insurance is truly designed for Long-term care… greater than 90 days. The benefits received are not considered taxable income. Tax qualified plans are **guaranteed renewable.** This means that your coverage can never be cancelled, as long as you pay your premiums.

Non-tax qualified plans allow the consumer to access benefits more quickly. With these plans, the insured only needs to prove that they require assistance with 1 out of 5 activities of daily living, with an attending physician's statement. Non-tax qualified plans are usually a bit more expensive than tax qualified. The jury is still out on whether or not the benefits are taxable as income. In the insurance world, there is a great debate on the pros and cons of each plan. Sticking with a tax-qualified plan is currently my recommendation.

PROPOSED TAX INCENTIVES IN 2003

There are essentially three federally proposed tax incentives. One is proposed by the House of Representatives (HR831), one is proposed by the Senate (S627), and one is proposed by President Bush.

HR831 and S627 both propose an above-the-line deduction, based on the following table, both for individual plans and workplace plans (otherwise known as "cafeteria" plans).

40 and younger = $250
41 – 50 = $470
51 – 60 = $940
61 – 70 = $2,510
71 and older = $3,130

President Bush, in 2002, proposed and above-the-line deduction based on the table shown above, however, the deduction would be:

25% in 2004,
35% in 2005,
65% in 2006,
And 100% in 2007.

President Bush's proposal does not include tax deductibility for workplace (cafeteria) plans.

THE CAREGIVER TAX CREDIT

The caregiver tax credit is being phased in over 4 years, and is equal to $3,000 per long-term care recipient that the caregiver is caring for. There are some limitations on that credit, which include reductions in the $3000 starting at $150,000 in adjusted gross income on a joint return, and $75,000 for an individual return.

Payment Options for Long-Term Care Insurance

ANNUAL PREMIUM PAYMENT

Annual premium payment means that the insured person will pay premiums for a lifetime or until they use their long-term care insurance. Payments can also be made monthly, quarterly, or semi-annually. Like auto or homeowners insurance, if payments are made on a monthly, quarterly, or semi-annual basis, there is usually an additional fee. Once the insured goes on claim most policies will waive the premium after the elimination period has been satisfied.

10-PAY

The 10-pay option allows the insured to pay a higher premium for a shorter period of time- 10 years. After 10 years of premium payment, no further premiums are due.

PAY TO 65

Some plans offer the option for the insured person to pay premiums until they are 65. At age 65, no further premium is due. This is a nice option because at retirement age, income may be significantly less than for working age adults.

LUMP SUM (ONE TIME) PAYMENT

Some consumers have the option to pay a one-time lump-sum premium. This means that no further premium is ever due. Many business owners find this option attractive for the tax deduction in the year that they purchase the policy. Asset based long-term care insurance is also a one time payment.

PAYING WITH INTEREST FROM AN ANNUITY

There is a way to pay for long-term care insurance without ever writing a check. Some consumers will assign the interest earned from an annuity to pay their annual premium.

REQUIRED MINIMUM DISTRIBUTION

At age 70 ? it is time to take the minimum distribution from an IRA or 401K. Some consumers may not need the extra income, and will use their minimum distribution to pay their annual long-term care insurance premium.

Non-Traditional Ways to Pay for Long-Term Care

ASSET BASED LONG-TERM CARE INSURANCE

There is another type of long-term care insurance available on the market today, that isn't regularly discussed, but is becoming increasingly popular. Asset based long-term care insurance combines life insurance and long-term care insurance. For instance, if a 65 year old non-smoking female had $50,000 sitting in a "rainy day" fund (CD or Money Market account), and does not need to use that money for income, she might want to transition that money to an asset based long-term care insurance plan so that it can work for her in many ways. If she transitions $50,000, she will have a death benefit of $104,000, OR a long-term care benefit of $310,000. If she dies and never needs long-term care, her heirs will receive twice what she put into the plan. If she needs long-term care, in this example, she will have 6 years worth of long-term care benefit available to her. Finally, if at some point she decides that she wants her $50,000 back to use for other purposes, she is always guaranteed the return of her principal (the amount she originally put in $50,000). This is a one time lump-sum payment to the insurance company, and no further premium is due. This type of plan is attractive for those consumers who want a return of their money even if they never need long-term care.

REVERSE MORTGAGES

There are different types of reverse mortgages. It is extremely important to investigate and find reputable lenders for this type of financing. When you do not qualify for traditional Long-Term Care Insurance there may be a need for cash flow to finance the cost of long-term care expenses.

Reverse mortgages do not change the ownership of the home. Therefore, you (the owner) are still responsible for taxes, maintenance, and homeowner's insurance. When the loan is over, the loan must be paid back by you, or your heirs, plus interest. A reputable lender will not want the house, they will want the loan repayment. Loan amounts available will depend on your age, and the value of your home. For more information on reverse mortgages reference the **"Aging Answers Rolodex"**.

LIFE SETTLEMENTS

A life settlement is the sale of a life insurance policy insuring the life of a senior citizen in return for a lump-sum of cash that is in excess of the policy's available cash values.

Most seniors over the age of 65 with a significant history of health problems can qualify for a senior settlement. Older seniors with no serious medical history may also participate. Most types of individual life insurance policies qualify, as long as they have been in-force for at least 2 years, and are at least $100,000 in face amount. The settlement amount will depend on several factors: your age, your current health situation, cost of your life insurance premiums and the size of your policy. This amount can only be determined once the life settlement company has reviewed all the information relating to the policy and the medical history of the insured. Once you transfer ownership of the policy you are no longer responsible for paying the premiums.

This strategy may also be helpful when cash flow is needed to finance the cost of long-term care. Very careful consideration should be given when choosing a life settlement company. Life settlements are different from Viaticals, but are a relatively new concept, and should be investigated thoroughly. Reference the **"Aging Answers Rolodex"** for resources and information.

Secret #5:
Long-Term Care Planning Includes Having Legal Documentation in Order

The fifth step to successful long-term care planning is:
Getting the right legal documents put together, so that when
you need care your family members can help you make
financial and care related decisions with peace of mind.
Expert legal assistance is essential.

Legal Matters

One of the most important things to set in motion is getting the legal paperwork taken care of! Power of Attorney for Health Care and Financial Power of Attorney are essential, along with an Advanced Directive or Living Will.

WHAT IS A "POWER OF ATTORNEY"?

Power of Attorney (POA) is a document whereby one person (called the "principal") authorizes another individual or entity (called an "agent" or "attorney-in-fact") to act on behalf of the principal. The most common uses for a POA are financial transactions and health care decisions. Most states have one set of laws governing financial POAs and second set of laws governing POAs for health care decisions. Therefore, it is the common and recommended practice not to mix the two purposes into one document. An individual desiring to have a POA covering both financial and medical situations should prepare two separate POAs, one dealing with financial issues and the second dealing with medical issues.

WHEN SHOULD I HAVE A FINANCIAL POWER OF ATTORNEY?

Persons with physical handicaps or limitations often set up financial POAs, with a family member as the agent, to the allow the family member to do such routine matters as making withdrawals from the principal's bank account. It would otherwise be a burden for the principal with physical limitations to make the short trip personally to perform the banking transaction. The second reason for preparation of a financial POA is preventative in nature. If you lose the mental capacity to handle your own financial affairs, without a durable power of attorney (see below), your family members will need to go to court and have a guardian or conservator appointed over your assets. If you have previously set up a durable power of attorney and then lose mental capacity, the agent named in your POA will be able to handle your financial affairs without the time and attorney fees necessary of going to the court to get a guardian and conservator appointed.

A **"Durable" POA** is one that remains in force even after the principal (i.e., the individual who executed the POA) loses mental capacity. Unless a POA is "durable", it will become ineffective at the time the principal becomes incompetent. Thus, a POA, which is not "durable", fails to protect you against the potential of your family having to go to court and get a guardian and conservator appointed over your assets.

WHAT MAKES A POWER OF ATTORNEY "DURABLE"?

This is a matter of state law. The Uniform Durable Power of Attorney Act has been adopted by 48 states and provides the following definition:

"A durable power of attorney is a power of attorney by which a principal, in writing, designates another as his attorney in fact and the writing contains the words, "This power of attorney shall not be affected by subsequent disability or incapacity of the principal", or "This power of attorney shall become effective upon the disability or incapacity of the principal", or similar words showing the intent of the principal that the authority conferred shall continue notwithstanding the subsequent disability or incapacity of the principal."

Therefore, the first requirement is that there be a written and signed document and second, the document contain words such as those above which clearly indicate that the principal intended the POA to be effective even after he or she became incapacitated. Although the language of the Uniform Act does not specifically state whether the document must also be notarized in order to be durable, the form recommended by the uniform laws commission has a space for the signature of a notary. Most states specially require POAs to be notarized to be durable and for them to be effective for real estate transactions. It is recommended that your POA be notarized. Also, some states require witnesses to the principal's signature.

ADVANCED DIRECTIVES (LIVING WILLS)

The term "advanced directives" refers to legal means by which individuals can express and, within certain limits, enforce their wishes regarding health care in the event that they become unconscious or otherwise mentally incapacitated. Common examples include living wills (which may direct families and physicians to withhold or withdraw life support if the person is terminally ill and permanently unconscious) and durable powers of attorney (which appoint and invest third parties with full authority to make decisions healthcare for incapacitated patients). When properly set up, these documents provide those who, in good faith, follow their provisions with protection from prosecution and civil suit.

LIVING TRUST

This is a trust created by an individual (the trustor), and administered by another party (the trustee) while the trustor is still alive. The individual creating the living trust can be his or her own trustee while they are living and not incapacitated. Upon the individual's death, a successor trustee named in the trust will become the administrator. A living trust can be either revocable or irrevocable. At the time of death, a living trust avoids probate in court and therefore gets assets of the estate distributed much more quickly and with less cost than a will does. It also offers a higher level of confidentiality, as probate proceedings are a matter of public record. Additionally, trusts are usually harder to contest than wills. On the downside, a living trust takes longer to put together than a will, and requires more ongoing maintenance. Although both a will and a living trust can be modified or revoked at any time before death, such changes are slightly more time-consuming for a living trust. Additionally, assets that a person wants to move to a living trust, such as real estate and bank or brokerage accounts, have to be retitled in the name of the trust. Will a living trust help you avoid spending down assets to qualify for Medicaid? Not likely. Consult an Elder Law Attorney for the regulations in your state.

Part Two

**Caring for an
Aging Parent
or Family Member**

Secret #1:
You Can Sometimes Stop the Financial Loss Associated with Medicaid "Spend Down!"

One of the most common mistakes that people make is in believing that they must "spend down" all of their assets to qualify for Medicaid. With proper financial planning and legal assistance, some estates can be fully or partially preserved, even after the aging adult is receiving long-term care.

Legal Assistance and Medicaid Planning – "Crisis Management"

Aging adults and their family members face certain challenging legal issues. Issues such as legal matters, financial matters, and care planning can be complicated for the potential nursing home resident, as well as for the family. Once again, expert legal help is often the key to solving many problems and avoiding future complexities. It is important to be able to identify a competent Elder Law Attorney who can assist the family in a timely and professional manner. Consumers should be cautious and check credentials thoroughly.

The leading national organization of Elder Law Attorneys is the National Academy of Elder Law Attorneys (NAELA), on the web at: *www.naela.org.* Membership is open to any lawyer, but the membership does show that at least the attorney has some interest in the field. Other sources to consider are referrals from family and friends, and referrals from other professionals such as social workers and medical professionals who work in long-term care. Ask the attorney how many nursing home cases they handle each month. It is likely that the attorney who does four Medicaid cases per month is more up to date than the attorney who does four per year.

Medicaid planning is certainly "crisis management" in long-term care. There are certain rules, regulations, and strategies that will allow a person to immediately qualify for Medicaid, without spending down all of their assets.

ONE EXAMPLE OF A STRATEGY

Strategies differ from state to state, but one common plan is to put some or all of a person's assets into a Medicaid Compliant Annuity. This will only work in states that determine eligibility based on assets, not in states that look at income.

The idea is that by using an immediate annuity that is Medicaid compliant, the person's assets are turned into an income stream, and therefore not counted as an asset.

Medicaid laws change every year, and get tighter and tighter as time goes on. So what may be possible today will probably not be possible in years to come. It is extremely important to hire an Elder Law Attorney who is familiar with current Medicaid law.

Is there hope that some assets can be preserved? Yes. In some cases a competent Elder Law Attorney and Financial Planner, working together, can stop the loss. This does not mean that it is appropriate to abuse the system, or put millionaires on Medicaid, but it does mean that there are certain laws set forth by each state that allow for some assets to be kept. There are multiple strategies available that the Division of Senior Services or Division of Family Services will not explain. For more information on contacting a competent Elder Law Attorney, use the "**Aging Answers Rolodex**" in the back of this book.

Secret #2:
Caring for an Aging Parent is Easier (But Never Easy) When the Caregiver is Caring for Themselves First

Successful caregiving starts with understanding that you are not alone, and that taking care of you, the caregiver, is just as important as caring for the aging adult.

One out of four families in the U.S. today are caring for an aging adult in some way. For some families, that means 24-hour live-in care. For other families, that means that Mom needs a ride to the doctor or to the grocery.

In the next 10-20 years it is projected that elder care will replace childcare as the number one issue for working adults.

Caring for an aging parent can be rewarding and overwhelming at the same time. After all, these are our parents. They raised us and cared for us. It's very difficult when the roles reverse.

When the Caregiver Needs a Break…
Where Can They Turn?

Caregivers of all kinds need a break now and then. So, where does a caregiver turn when they are feeling stressed out, tired, emotionally drained, or overwhelmed?

RESPITE CARE

Respite (*res-* pit) care is often the answer. Respite care is ***time off*** for the caregiver. Respite gives you (the caregiver) time away to rest and do necessary activities so that you can continue to provide good care for your loved one. Often, being a caregiver is a job that can be physically and emotionally draining. Without relief, your physical and emotional health can be affected, reducing the quality of care for your family member. There are several options when it comes to respite care.

In-home care can be arranged for as little as a few hours, up to several days with the proper planning and financial resources. Be sure to pick an agency with a great reputation and proven reliability. Make sure that background checks are done on all employees and Elder/Child Abuse checks are also completed. In-home care for long periods of time can be costly, so be sure to budget for the expense. Also, many home health agencies require several days or weeks of advance notice for long assignments. Plan ahead!

Nursing Home/ Assisted Living facilities often will offer respite care for a weekend or a full week or more. Many facilities have a minimum number of days required. The cost includes room and board. Many other services will be extra. Some facilities will only require a few days notice, and others will require several weeks' notice. Check with the facilities in your area for costs and bed availability. Again, as always, it is important to plan ahead.

Local Area Agencies on Aging or Social Service Agencies will sometimes sponsor programs that allow for volunteers to come to the home and provide respite care for short periods of time. These visits are usually just for a few hours. The volunteers are not medical professionals and therefore are not able to care for seriously ill family members, but they are able to provide some relief! These programs are usually free or at a very low cost to local residents. Contact your local Area Agency on Aging for more information. Consult the "**Aging Answers Rolodex**" in the back of the book.

The Alzheimer's Association is a great source of information. You don't have to be taking care of an Alzheimer's diagnosed family member to take advantage of their referral database. Your local agency can usually provide you with a wealth of information, resources and contacts. Consult the "**Aging Answers Rolodex**" in the back of the book.

Family and friends are a great resource for the caregiver. Don't be afraid to ask for help. Many people are happy to assist with errand running and caregiving. Have a family meeting and ask each family member for 1-2 hours of his or her time per week. This will allow you to take a hot bath, read a book, go for a much-needed walk, or just go shopping. Make a schedule and give each family member a copy.

Local Churches and Other Organizations are generally willing to send volunteers out to the home for a few hours. Again, most of these volunteers are non-medical personnel and will only be able to stay for a couple of hours at a time.

Taking care of yourself is just as important as caring for your disabled/ aging family member. If you become ill, what will happen to your loved one? Don't hesitate to ask for help. If you look in the right places you might find more help than you need.

So, take a much-needed break. You deserve it!

Hospice Care – At The End of Life

Hospice care is end of life care. Usually, it is estimated by a physician that a patient has 6 months or less to live. Hospice focuses on caring for the individual, keeping them comfortable, and providing support for the family. Hospice care can be provided in the home, in a free-standing facility, or in a long-term care facility. These services are available to patients of all ages. It is covered under Medicare, Medicaid, and most private insurance plans. Long-Term Care Insurance also covers hospice care.

The primary caregiver for a hospice patient is usually a family member. There is a team of healthcare professionals available to help the primary caregiver. This team often includes a physician, a registered nurse, home health aids, clergy or social services, trained volunteers, and physical or occupational therapists. Traditional insurance plans like Medicare and private health insurance will cover needed supplies, equipment, and licensed healthcare practitioners like nurses and physical therapists. However, when a family needs 24 hour care provided by a home health aid, or other unlicensed personnel, they end up paying privately for this service or utilize their long-term care insurance benefits. Most long-term care insurers provide hospice care as a standard benefit in their plan and there is no need to meet the elimination period.

Secret #3:
Living at Home is Possible, and A Lot Easier When You Know What Questions to Ask!

Successful caregiving continues with knowing how to "talk the talk" of home care providers and adult day care centers. Don't be afraid to ask questions, and don't be satisfied until you get the right answers.

Tips and Hints for Choosing In-Home Care Services

- Be Organized.
- Ask the Home Care Agency if they have a back-up person on-call in case of caregivers becoming ill, or not showing up.
- Provide the aide with a checklist of duties for EACH DAY.
- The aide should not sleep, or smoke in your home.
- If there is a problem, immediately contact the agency that sent the aide.
- The aides should provide their own lunch/dinner unless you offer.
- Do not tip.

- Do not send your loved one out in a car with the aide unless this situation is prearranged with the agency.
- Aides should not use the phone for lots of personal calls.
- Make sure you know in advance how payment is expected.
- Some aides are Certified Nurse's Aides (CNAs) and others are not. Some will take a blood pressure and a pulse, others will not. Ask the agency.
- There should be some consistency after about 1 to 2 weeks regarding the person who is sent to the home. Sometimes it takes a week or so to get the same person on the schedule for your home. Be patient!
- What is the hiring practice of the agency? Have background checks been performed on every caregiver? What about Elder Abuse or Child Abuse database checks? Are they bonded and insured?
- If there are too many late shows/no shows or inconsistencies, CHANGE AGENCIES (speak to them about the problem first, perhaps they can correct the situation).

Medical vs. Non-Medical Home Care Services

There are two different types of home care providers, **medical** and **non-medical**. A non-medical home care agency supplies caregivers who will do household chores such as light cleaning, laundry, errand running, grocery shopping, picking up prescriptions, light meal preparation, and getting the mail. They will also provide services that help with socialization and transportation like accompanying the aging adult to a doctor's appointment, sitting and watching TV together, playing card games or board games, taking the senior to special events or senior centers, going to the library, and other social activities.

Medical home care providers can assist with many of these things, but also provide bathing and dressing assistance, medication reminders, and assistance with transferring from the bed to a chair.

No one can take care of your parent or spouse exactly the way you would, but a good agency will provide caring and compassionate staff who do the best job they can. The squeaky wheel always gets the grease when it comes to service providers. Do your homework prior to hiring an agency, and be sure to check on your aging loved one regularly. Visit unexpectedly, and monitor what's happening in the home. Speak up and communicate with the agency!

Adult Day Care

Adult Day Care Centers are becoming a popular alternative to nursing home placement. They offer the ability for the elderly to spend the day in an enriching environment, full of social activities and learning opportunities. Many Adult Day Centers will provide transportation to and from the center for an extra charge. Meals are provided, as well as medication administration. Day trips, crafts, computer stations, libraries, and music are often part of the overall experience. Some Adult Day Centers will take Medicaid, but most prefer private pay. This allows the senior to live at home with another member of the family, but have supervision and social interaction during the day while family members are at work.

Tips for Choosing an Adult Day Care Center

- Identify services in your area. For names and phone numbers of the adult day centers, try:
- Yellow Pages ("Adult Day Care;" "Aging Services;" Senior Citizens' Services," etc.)
- Area Agency on Aging (AAA) Call 1-800-677-1116 for the AAA in your area, or search for them online. See the **"Aging Answers Rolodex".**
- A local senior center
- Your family doctor
- A Geriatric Care Manager

- Call first! Call adult day centers and ask for a flier or brochure, eligibility criteria, a monthly activity calendar, a monthly menu and application procedures.

- Know what to ask. Look for the following information:
- Owner or sponsoring agency.
- Years of operation.
- License or certification (If required in your state).
- Hours of operation.
- Days open.
- Transportation
- Cost – Hourly or daily charge, other charges, financial assistance.
- Conditions accepted – such as memory loss, limited mobility, and incontinence.
- Staff credentials.
- Number of staff per participant.
- Activities provided – Is there variety and choice of individual and group activities?
- Menu – appeal, balance.
- Tour. After reviewing materials, make an appointment to visit two or more centers that might meet your needs.
- Check references. Talk to two or three people who have used the center you are considering. Ask for their opinion.
- Try it out. Select a day center. Try it for three to five days. It sometimes takes several visits for new participants to feel comfortable in a new setting and with a new routine. If you have questions or are experiencing any problems, ask for a conference. The staff may have suggestions to make the transition easier both at home and at the day center.

Secret #4:
Alternative Living Arrangements Can Be a Positive Experience

Successful caregiving also means knowing what alternative living arrangements are available. Many seniors decide to make lifestyle changes that will promote their independence and give them flexible options when it comes to actually needing care. Keep in mind that although some average costs are listed below, this is for room and board only. Additional services, medications, and supplies can cost 20% more per day above the basic room and board charges.

Continuum Of Care
Retirement Communities (CCRC)

A CCRC is a community for seniors that encompasses all levels of care, from independent living, to assisted living, to nursing home care, all on one campus. Some couples and single seniors will move to a CCRC for various reasons including simplifying their lifestyle, no longer having to worry about lawn and house maintenance, and increased social activity with people of their own generation. Independent living offers an apartment or town-home with access to 1-2 meals per day in a restaurant style setting, recreational activities, group tours and day outings, and transportation to doctor appointments and grocery stores. They often include walking trails, workout rooms, computer labs, libraries, chapels, and small convenient stores. The independent portion of a CCRC is not considered long-term care; it is simply a lifestyle choice. Independent senior living has a cost range of $1100-$3000 per month. Most cities do have Section 8 or HUD housing specifically for seniors. Sometimes there is a waiting list for subsidized housing. Check the **"Aging Answers Rolodex"** in the back of the book.

Assisted Living Facilities

Sometimes, on the same campus there are assisted living facilities that offer most of the same accommodations, but with a little more assistance and structure. In an assisted living facility each resident typically has their own apartment, but without a kitchenette. They are served 3 meals per day in a family style or restaurant style setting. Medication delivery is available, as well as linen service, laundry service, housekeeping, and assistance with bathing and dressing if needed. Again, recreational and social activities, and transportation is also provided.

There are stand-alone assisted living facilities that are not associated with CCRCs. Assisted living is becoming the most popular form of long-term care, and is seen as a transition between independent living and nursing home care. This is a nice option for people who need some extra help, but are not ready for full 24-hour care. Cost for Assisted Living ranges from $1900-$3500 per month.

Nursing Home Care

When independent or assisted living is no longer a viable option, a nursing home will provide 24-hour care by trained and licensed staff. A Registered Nurse or Licensed Practical Nurse is on duty at all times. Some nursing homes are private pay only, some take Medicare, and some will accept Medicaid as payment for services. Most residents live in a semi-private room, (private if they can afford it) and are allowed to decorate with their own personal belongings. There are new trends in nursing home care called The Eden Alternative™. These programs incorporate living things like plants, animals, and children into residential care facilities to make them more like a home, rather than an institution for the frail and elderly. The average cost for a semi-private nursing home bed nationwide is around $150.00 per day ($4,500 per month) or more. For more information on The Eden Alternative™, see the "**Aging Answers Rolodex**".

Tips for Choosing an Assisted Living or Nursing Care Facility

Choosing a facility for a loved one, or even for yourself, can often be difficult and time consuming. The following tips and hints will help give you guidance when trying to make that decision. Remember – take notes on each facility you visit, and compare them later.

- Speak with people you trust about their experiences with Nursing Homes.
- Pick a good LOCATION.
- Ask the home about BED AVAILABILITY.
- Do they have Medicare, Medicaid, or Private Pay beds available?
- What is the STAFFING ARRANGMENT? RNS? LPNS? CNAS?
- Are there extra services and fees?
- Is the home able to provide for special care needs such as Alzheimer's, End Stage Renal Disease, or other medical conditions?
- VISIT THE HOMES ON YOUR LIST! Nothing replaces a tour.
- Ask to see a copy of the most recent state inspection. Or visit the Nursing Home Compare site on the web. www.medicare.gov (see "**Aging Answers Rolodex**" in the back of the book).
- Do the residents seem to have a good quality of life?
- How long has the current staff been working at the facility?

- Does the facility do background checks for criminal and elder abuse activity prior to hiring them?
- Upon entering the facility, pay attention to what you SEE and what you SMELL.
- What are the visiting hours?
- Be sure to visit the home at least once when they are not expecting you.
- Make an inventory of the items that you or your loved one brings to the home for future reference.
- Talk to some of the other visitors/ family members. How do they feel about the care provided?

Secret #5:
There Are Professionals Who Help Families With These Issues and Decisions Every Day

Geriatric Care Managers are a valuable resource in every community. Many people have never heard of geriatric care management, but it is an emerging and important profession.

Geriatric Care Management as a Resource

When faced with decisions regarding long-term care for an aging loved one, a geriatric care manager may be one of the best private resources in your area. A geriatric care manager has extensive knowledge of all local resources related to aging and caregiving, as well as family and personal issues and concerns.

Geriatric care managers can be located nationwide. They assist with coordination of care for aging and disabled adults.

This service is provided in a series of steps including initial assessment, care plan development, implementation of services, and quality of care monitoring. Geriatric care managers are typically nurses, social workers, gerontologists, physical therapists, occupational therapists, or other social service professionals.

The "care management" process can improve the quality of life not only for the aging adult, but also for the caregivers and family members involved. The service is very personalized and utilizes the same principals of "case management".

Most geriatric care managers are available to the family and client 24 hours per day, 7 days per week. The ultimate goal is to keep the aging adult in the home for as long as **safely** possible. In-home care can be arranged at any level of need to accommodate the client and the family. Geriatric care managers often will be asked to arrange other services for the client such as bill paying, housekeeping, lawn care, transportation to appointments, grocery shopping, meal delivery, and personal care issues.

When the client is in need of transition to alternative living arrangements like nursing home, assisted living, or even independent retirement communities, the care manager often can recommend the best facilities that meet the clients financial needs.

Geriatric Care Management is truly a holistic approach to caring for the aging adult. All resources available are utilized to assist families when long-term care is needed.

Care managers are also often asked to troubleshoot quality concerns with nursing homes and home care agencies. Their level of professionalism and knowledge of the local regulations and laws are of great value to the family. They are considered "advocates" for the elderly.

Geriatric care management is paid for privately by client and family members, Medicare and Medicaid do not cover these services. However, Long-Term Care Insurance does cover some or all of the care management fee.

Most geriatric care managers belong to the National Association of Professional Geriatric Care Managers. In order to find a care manager in your area, you can search for one through their website at www.caremanager.org (See the **"Aging Answers Rolodex"**).

In the Midwest, you can search for a local care manager at www.midwestgcm.org, or for an example of a specific care management website, try www.seniorcaresolutionsinc.com.

Geriatric care management services save the family both time and money, and ultimately decrease the stress and frustration of the caregiver. The process gives the family and the aging adult the opportunity to make informed and appropriate decisions regarding any long-term care needs.

Recommendations for Choosing a Geriatric Care Manager

Choosing a geriatric care manager is much like choosing any other professional that you and your family would be working with closely.

- Look for a member of the National Association of Professional Geriatric Care Managers. These members have met certain criteria regarding education and experience in health sciences, and social service.
- Ask for References.
- Ask for literature about their company, years of practice, websites, and biography.
- Check with the Better Business Bureau.
- Ask about fees, contracts, and extra charges like mileage or phone calls.
- Be sure you understand what services they provide, and their on-call schedule. Will they be available 24 hours a day?
- Remember that a geriatric care manager becomes your "eyes and ears", especially when you live some distance from your parents. Ask them about their process, their communication schedule (Will they report daily, weekly, or monthly?) Is the primary communication via telephone or email?

- Communicate any concerns immediately, and work together as a team to accomplish the ultimate goal, which is keeping your loved one safe, and well cared for.

My Parent Doesn't Want Any Help! What Should I Do?

Perhaps you have noticed that Mom or Dad isn't bathing regularly, or the bills aren't being paid, or the house is uncharacteristically messy. Maybe they seem to forget directions from one location to anther, or even worse, they have had a car accident, or report falling in the home when no one was around to help them. Often, adult children of aging parents notice changes in their loved ones, and when the aging adult is confronted with the facts, they say, "Oh everything is fine, I don't need any help, don't worry about me!"

The loss of independence and choice is something none of us want to face. Having our own children tell us what do to or how to live our lives is uncomfortable at best. Many aging adults are also very private about their financial matters, and will not discuss income or assets with adult children.

How do you start that conversation with your parents? There is not a one-size-fits-all answer. Below are some tips that might help the process along.

Pick an appropriate time and place. Avoid large family gatherings, holidays, birthdays, and other celebrations. A quiet location, in their home or yours might be more comfortable.

Avoid blaming or accusing. Instead, redirect the conversation by telling your parent how YOU feel. For example, "Mom, I find myself worrying about you a lot these days, and I would like to tell you why I am feeling this way."

Talk to a geriatric care manager in your area for some good advice on how to approach your parent's specific needs. That care manager has helped family members have this kind of conversation hundreds of times throughout their career. They are full of helpful hints and tips.

If you decide to seek the services of a geriatric care manager, ask them about their approach when it comes to dealing with difficult clients, or clients who may not perceive a need for services.

I often tell adult children that when they approach their parents about setting up an evaluation, they might tell their parents, "I know you don't want me to worry about you, and I only want the best for you. Having this professional come over and talk to us would really make me feel better. If you would agree to talk with her, we can look at her recommendations together and see if any of them make sense. Is that fair?"

Remember that having a third party, who is not a family member and is completely objective, can help the senior see things from a different point of view. They feel like they are getting some professional advice, as opposed to opinions from their children.

Finally, if the senior is truly not living safely, a geriatric care manager can let the senior know that they need to make some choices about their care or living arrangements NOW, before someone else has to make that decision for them later. Of course, this is done with professionalism, courtesy, compassion, and caring.

Secret #6:
Other Families Have Written to Ask For Help, You Are Not Alone.

The following are some of the most common questions asked by caregivers from across the country, and one particular family's struggle, as told by the oldest daughter.

Questions and Answers

Q. Recently my father was in the hospital, in the ICU, on a ventilator… very sick for several days. My brothers and sisters and I had some very difficult discussions about what to do in the event that he did not fully recover. We don't think he would want to be on a breathing machine for life. Now he has recovered, but what can we do to avoid this conflict in the future. None of us really want to make that decision for him.

A. The answer is never simple, but the first thing I would recommend is having your father fill out an Advanced Directive, or Living Will. These forms will help the family understand exactly what his requests are for end of life care. Every area hospital carries the information needed to complete the paperwork. Or you can go online and find the forms yourself. Planning ahead for these situations is always our best bet;

otherwise we end up managing a crisis, which is something none of us need to be doing when a loved one is critically ill.

Q. My mother has recently moved in with us due to her failing health and forgetfulness. I am no longer able to leave her in our home alone during the day. What options do I have? I am uncomfortable with having a stranger in my home (like a home health aid).

A. Adult Day Care may be a very possible option for your family. There are many centers located in most metropolitan areas. Costs may vary, but in general will be much less expensive than having a home health aid in the house for 8 hours per day.

Q. What is the best way to evaluate a nursing home, and choose one that meets my father's needs? Our family is really struggling with this issue. Are there any resources that can help?

A. There are several resources available that can help a family make the right decision the first time around. First, you might want to visit www.medicare.gov. This website will allow the consumer to search for nursing homes by state and zip code. You can view demographics, staffing ratios, and the last state survey for each home listed. This will give you an idea of any difficulties the home may be having, and will help you start compiling a list of questions. Second, I recommend touring the homes you select (narrow it down to about 3). There is no substitute for actually visiting a home that you are considering. Ask questions; visit with family members who are there with their loved ones. Ask them how THEY feel about the care being provided. Finally, Geriatric Care Managers who work in your local area are always a good resource for information on local facilities. You can find a Geriatric Care Manager at www.caremanager.org. Search for one by state or zip code.

Q. My aunt is 79 years old, and in fairly good health. She has no children of her own. She would like to re-do her will, update her living trust, and have me listed as Power of Attorney. What does Power of Attorney mean, and what kind of responsibility I am taking on?

A. Power of Attorney can be for health care, or financial, or both. Most likely if she trusts you, she will have you designated as both healthcare and financial POA. This means that in the event that she cannot make decisions for herself due to cognitive or physical impairment, you would be able to act on her behalf. You would be making decisions regarding some of her care needs, and paying her bills, and managing her investments or assets. This is a simplified explanation. I think it is a wonderful idea to have these documents in place prior to the crisis of acute illness, or declining health due to age. She should be getting her "ducks in a row", so to speak long before she becomes ill. Unfortunately, too many people do nothing at all or wait until it's too late to get their affairs in order. These types of documents are a form of pre-planning, and something I highly advocate. You will have to decide if this is a responsibility that you are willing to accept.

Q. My parents are considering moving to an Assisted Living Facility because my father is in poor health, and could use the extra assistance. Do you have any recommendations? What should we be looking for in this type of facility?

A. Assisted Living Facilities are a nice transition from a completely independent environment, to one that offers extra support, while maintaining some level of independence. Many senior couples will consider this option if they want to stay together, but one is requiring more supervision or assistance with activities of daily living. Most Licensed Facilities will require that each individual is able to "negotiate the pathway to safety", meaning that they can exit the building in a timely manner during an emergency (such as fire) without the assistance of another person. Take the time to tour a few facilities in your parents' area, look at their last state inspection results, and ask about pricing. "Extras" like laundry service, bath visits (assistance with bathing), prescription drug reminders, and supplies may cost more. Just as with any transition to a facility, it is important that the family and the senior do their homework. Investigate the different options that are available, and become an informed consumer before making that move!

Q. My parent has been diagnosed with Alzheimer's disease. I am certain that we will have to place him in a nursing home in the next few months. The decision is agonizing and heartbreaking. How do other people get through this, and where do I turn to for support and guidance?

A. I get this question a lot. There are no easy answers. Since this is an issue that so many people struggle with, I decided it would be most helpful to interview a caregiver, someone who has "been there". Deborah Glover-Uetz, is the author of *Into the Mist, When Someone You Love Has Alzheimer's Disease*; her co-author is Dr. Anne Lindsay, Neurophysiologist. Deborah's father was diagnosed with Alzheimer's disease in 1999. She had the help of her two brothers and her mother, as they struggled to make the best decisions and choices regarding his care. Their father passed away in March of 2002. Deborah's book has not gone to print, but when it is published, we will update everyone. So, in her own words…

What prompted you to write about your experience?

The book began as my journal. I found it very helpful and therapeutic to write about what was happening as my father was battling Alzheimer's disease. As I began to search for information I was left wanting to know more. I could find books that touched on topics but nothing that told the whole story. I decided that I wanted to write a book that would answer the questions my family had and help those who would go through the experience after us. I never dreamed I would become friends with Dr. Andre Delacourte, a leading research scientist in France, and even have my writing featured on the INSERM web page. INSERM is the Institute of Health in Lille France.

Describe some of your trials and tribulations as a caregiver.

Throughout the care giving experience you second-guess your decisions. You ask yourself "what would my loved one do if it were me?" You find yourself trying to hang on to anything that might indicate a wrong diagnosis. Accepting that it is in fact Alzheimer's disease is very hard to do. As each day dawns there are new challenges. Just as the title suggests you feel as if you are in a mist and with each step forward the mist closes in behind you. It takes a team to handle the ever-changing situation as you do your best to keep your loved one safe and to keep yourself from becoming burned out. You must be sure your loved one is safe in their own home, as they no longer recognize their surroundings. As the disease progresses falls become a primary concern. Many Alzheimer's patients are awake all night and must be supervised to insure they don't wander away from the home. The job of a caregiver is so taxing that it is best handled by a family team if possible.

How did your family work as a team?

Each of us did what we were best at. Some sat by Dad's bedside for hours and talked about his life and made him smile. Others tackled the legal issues and paperwork that seemed endless. We all gave all that we could and did the best that we knew how. I think each of us feels like we have nothing to regret regarding our role in his care.

Is there anything you would have done differently?

Hindsight is an amazing thing. As I look back there are a few things I would have done that I didn't do. I would have asked Dad more about his life while he was able to talk to me. I don't think I really had accepted that our time to share in conversation would pass so quickly. I would have talked to him about Alzheimer's. I wonder now if he would have liked to have someone to discuss it with. We were all afraid of mentioning it in front of him because we didn't want to upset him or scare him. I would have been a more informed consumer when it came time to choose a nursing home.

Any words of wisdom for current caregivers?

My words of wisdom for current caregivers would be reach out for help. Don't be embarrassed by the things your loved one may say or do. They are ill and people will understand. Seek the help of friends, your church, social services, and if possible, a geriatric care manager. The job of caregiver is too big for one person regardless your age or background. Eventually you will need help and you shouldn't wait until the disease has taken a physical and mental toll on you along with your loved one. Go to local support groups or support groups on line.

Describe how your family was affected by the experience.

My mother was exhausted but wouldn't slow down and take care of herself. After my dad was placed in a nursing home she finally had a moment to see her doctor. It was discovered she had cancer. If she had not seen the doctor she would most likely have died before Dad. She pulled up all the strength she had left and followed through with surgery. She is now cancer free. My brothers and I have all been affected by Dad's battle. We miss him more than we expected. We knew we would miss him of course, but we didn't realize that as he became more like an infant, the feeling of being so responsible for him was so endearing. He was our baby. He depended upon us for every bite we spoon-fed him. We tucked him in at night and smothered him with kisses. When he died we were holding his hand. I wouldn't wish him back for anything because I know he is finally at peace but I would love one more hug.

Advice on nursing home placement?

You will know if the time comes that you can no longer provide the care your loved one needs. Don't look upon this as a personal failure. I would advise you not to wait until you hit that point before you explore your options. Choosing a nursing home is perhaps the most important decision you will make. Your loved one will depend upon the quality of care they provide for their every need. Visit the nursing homes you are considering UNANNOUNCED. Visit during meal times and be certain you see the nursing home on a weekend. A nursing home will be at its best if you make an appointment and have a marketing representative show you the facility. It will be at its worst on a weekend when there is less staff and fewer activities. As you visit the nursing home ask some of the residents if they like living there. Don't base your decision on one reply but ask several. If there are family members visiting their loved ones ask them their opinion of the facility. Every nursing home has to have a state survey and the results of that survey are supposed to be kept in plain sight, usually in the lobby area. Read the survey.

Once you decide upon a specific nursing home ask to see the room where your loved one will reside. Don't settle for looking at a similar room. When you are in the room do you hear residents shouting? If you do, ask to see a room on a different hall. It is a common practice to show a perspective client the quietest hall and a beautiful room but that may not be anything like where your loved one is placed. Do your homework before you are up against a time crunch.

What was your greatest form of support?

My greatest support throughout Dad's illness was my faith in God. My greatest earthly support was oddly enough two people I have never met face to face. Rose Steele, whose father's story is one of those featured in my book, resides in Australia. We "met" in an online support group sponsored by Massachusetts General Hospital. Rose and I continued to correspond after her father passed away. We have spoken by phone many times and I treasure her friendship more than I can even explain. Dr. Anne Lindsay, daughter of John Lindsay, former mayor of New York City, is a neurophysiologist whom I also met during my research of the disease. She is now my co-writer and my dear friend. I think God has put these people in my path and the book will be greatly enriched thanks to both of them. My husband Edward and my daughters, son-in-laws and grandchildren were all a source of strength and joy.

I would never have believed that when I started a journal of my father's illness it would grow into a book and include the life stories of Dad and two other Alzheimer's patients, and have sections written by two world-renowned research scientists and a neurophysiologist. I consider every person's contribution to my book a treasure, and it will be such a source of information and comfort to those who are just entering into the mist.

Deborah Glover-Uetz can be contacted by email at dlgu@charter.net.

Conclusion

We have lived with the myths of long-term care long enough. We believe that it will never happen to us, that our current health insurance plan will pay for it, and that planning ahead is too expensive and difficult. The reality is: chances are we WILL need long-term care, our current health insurance was NEVER designed to pay for it, and NOT planning ahead is more expensive and difficult than taking a proactive approach.

Most of us would like to live a long, healthy life. But with a long healthy life comes a series of decisions and possible complications that need to be addressed before it's too late. Long-term care is not a topic that is easily discussed on Sunday afternoon, with the family gathered around the kitchen table. In fact, discussing long-term care and planning ahead for long-term care has been, and continues to be, one of America's least favorite things to do.

The intention of this book is to help families start that conversation and unravel the myths of long-term care. It doesn't matter whether you are a 30-something, a baby-boomer, or a 70-something... long-term care is a family matter. It affects all of us. It affects our personal lives, and our careers. We may be the 30-something faced with caring for an aging parent, or we may be a baby-boomer trying to decide the best way to plan ahead. For anyone who has been approached about the need for long-term care insurance, and for anyone who has had a long-term care "experience" in their family, this book was designed to turn myth into reality, and provide useful common-sense information from a healthcare professional who has worked on both sides of the long-term care continuum.

It is important to understand that longevity, changes in family structure, changes in the workplace, and the insurance industry in general, all have contributed to the need for pre-planning.

Planning ahead for long-term care requires a proactive approach and a positive attitude.

People who plan ahead, do so for various reasons, including:

- To protect and preserve assets for themselves, and their children.
- Wanting to maintain independence and choice.
- Wanting to receive quality care.
- Not wanting to be a burden to their family members.
- Not wanting to end up impoverished and on Medicaid.

For others, the situation is a bit different. Long-term care is already happening, or HAS happened. There was no time to plan ahead, or it just wasn't done. Therefore, family members are faced with trying to provide the best care, in the best circumstances possible.

The Message

The message is clear. Understanding the secrets to long-term care planning, caregiving, and crisis management, is essential for all families across America. Planning ahead for long-term care has never been more important. We are on the verge of an exploding aging population (76,000,000 aging baby-boomers!). The Medicaid system is a disaster. It is imperative to understand that long-term care is not a matter of entitlement. Long-term care IS the responsibility of each individual. How we plan ahead, how we pay for it, and how and where we are cared for, is up to each one of us.

In 2002, the federal government sent it's own clear message to over 20 million people. As an employer, the federal government offered group long-term care insurance to all employees, active military, retired federal employees, retired military, their spouses, adult children, step-children, adopted children, parents, and parents-in-law. This program was implemented and offered as voluntary enrollment, with no contributions of premium by the federal government. Why? Because the U.S. Office of Personnel Management knows that in the next ten to twenty years, our healthcare systems will be overburdened and under-funded (they already are!). They have encouraged federal employees and military personnel to take an active role in their own long-term care planning. To date, the program has been very successful.

Families who are now faced with caring for an aging parent or relative, need resources and information that will assist them in making the best decisions possible regarding care. If your parent or aging loved one is in need of services, or is currently in a long-term care crisis, there is hope. Educating ourselves about services that are currently available is imperative, and makes the journey much easier for the entire family.

Hear the message before it is too late. Do something rather than nothing at all. Not making a decision, is a decision in itself. Be an informed consumer, and make a choice that will not only affect you personally, but will allow your family members the opportunity for peace of mind down the road.

The Aging Answers Rolodex

The following pages contain informational websites, phone numbers, and addresses of organizations and companies who help with a variety of aging issues. Many will have a local chapter or affiliate near you.

Financial Planning Assistance

WEALTH PROTECTION ADVISORS, LLC
Asset Preservation and Long-Term Care
1401 Triad Center Drive
St. Peters, MO 63376
636-441-3700
www.shopltc.com
www.gsainfo.org

Be sure to mention that you heard about Wealth Protection in the Aging Answers Book! Ask for Don Quante, CSA; or talk to his Operations Manager Barb Bott.

THE FINANCIAL PLANNING ASSOCIATION – FPA
5775 Glenridge Drive, NE, Suite B-300
Atlanta, GA 30328
www.fpanet.org

NATIONAL ASSOCIATION OF PERSONAL FINANCIAL ADVISORS – NAPFA
355 W. Dundee Rd. Suite 200
Buffalo Grove, IL 60089
888-FEE-ONLY
www.napafa.org

SOCIETY OF FINANCIAL SERVICE PROFESSIONALS – SFSP
270 S. Bryn Mawr Ave.
Bryn Mawr, PA 19010
888-243-2258
www.finacialpro.org

NATIONAL CENTER FOR HOME EQUITY CONVERSION – NCHEC
360 N. Robert St., #403
St. Paul, MN 55101
800-209-8085
www.reverse.org

Information on reverse mortgages, and how hey can be used to fund long-term care costs!

COVENTRY CORPORATE CENTER – LIFE SETTLEMENT INFORMATION
7111 Valley Green Road
Fort Washington, PA 19034
T: 877 836 8300 / 215 233 5100
F: 215 233 3201
E: info@coventryfirst.com
www.coventryfirst.com

"Coventry First is recognized as the serious, top tier professional firm in the life settlement industry. Our principals have been involved in sophisticated high net worth and corporate markets for more than 20 years. Our affiliated companies have placed and serviced more than $11 billion of life insurance with aggregate premiums totaling more than $1 billion and have delivered more than $110 million in death claims since 1990." – *coventryfirst.com*

———————————————————————

WEISS RATINGS, INC.
4176 Burns Road
Palm Beach Gardens, FL 33410
800-289-9222
www.weissratings.com

Financial ratings on Long-Term Care Insurance companies can be found here.

———————————————————————

Long-Term Care Insurance/ Health Insurance

NATIONAL ASSOCIATION OF INSURANCE COMMISSIONERS – NAIC
Hall of States
444 North Capitol Street, NW
Suite 701
Washington, DC 20001-1512
202-624-7790 (Voice)
202-624-3540 (FAX, Government/Media Relations)
202-624-8579 (FAX, Washington Counsel)
www.naic.org

Publishes the "Shopper's Guide to Long-Term Care Insurance", available at their website for download, or ordering.

HEALTH INSURANCE ASSOCIATION OF AMERICA, PUBLIC AFFAIRS
DEPARTMENT – HIAA
555 13TH ST., NW
SUITE 600
WASHINGTON, DC 20004
202-824-1600 (VOICE)
202-824-1722 (VOICE)
www.hiaa.org

HEALTH INSURANCE ASSOCIATION OF AMERICA – HIAA
1201 F St., NW, Suite 500
Washington, DC 20004-1109
800-879-4422
www.hiaa.org

"The Health Insurance Association of America (HIAA®) is the voice of America's health insurers, who protect consumers from the financial risks of illness and injury by providing flexible and affordable products and services that embody freedom of choice." – *hiaa.org*

LONG-TERM CARE INSURANCE EDUCATIONAL FOUNDATION
PO BOX 370
Centerville, VA 20122
www.ltcedfoundation.org

"The Long-Term Care Insurance Educational Foundation is a nonprofit 501(c) 3 organization. Its purpose is to plan and execute a national conference focused on public policy issues affecting the development of the private long-term care insurance market." – *ltcedfoundation.org*

⊸ ———————————————————— ⊷

Various Long-Term Care Insurance Companies

GENERAL ELECTRIC CAPITAL ASSURANCE COMPANY
LONG-TERM CARE DIVISION
1650 Los Gamos Dr.
San Rafael, CA 94903
800-456-7766
www.gefn.com/longtermcare

⊸ ———————————————————— ⊷

JOHN HANCOCK FINANCIAL SERVICES
200 CLARENDON ST.
BOSTON, MA 02117
800-695-7389
www.jhancock.com

⊸ ———————————————————— ⊷

METROPOLITAN LIFE INSURANCE COMPANY (METLIFE)
LONG-TERM CARE GROUP
PO BOX 937
Westport, CT 06881-0937
800-308-0179
www.metlife.com

PHYSICIANS MUTUAL INSURANCE COMPANY
2600 Dodge St.
Omaha, NE 68131
www.pmic.com

TRANSAMERICA OCCIDENTAL LIFE INSURANCE COMPANY
(MEMBER OF THE AEGON INSURANCE GROUP)
2705 Brown Trail
Bedford, TX 76021
800-227-3740
www.transamerica.com

Government Agencies of Interest

DEPARTMENT OF VETERANS AFFAIRS (VA)
810 Vermont Ave. NW
Washington, DC 20420
800-827-1000
www.va.gov

PARALYZED VETERANS OF AMERICA (PVA)
VETERANS BENEFITS DEPT.
801 18th St., NW
Washington, DC 20006
800-424-8200
www.pva.org

CENTERS FOR MEDICARE & MEDICAID SERVICES (CMS)
Region VII
Richard Bolling Federal Building
Room 235
601 East 12th Street
Kansas City, Missouri 64106
Phone: (816) 426-5233
www.medicare.gov

- Nursing Home Compare
- Medigap Compare
- Medicare Health Plan Compare
- Dialysis Facility Compare
- Helpful Contacts
- Participating Provider Directory
- Prescription Drug Assistance Programs
- Supplier Directory

CENTERS FOR MEDICARE AND MEDICAID SERVICES (CMS),
FORMERLY THE HEALTH CARE FINANCING ADMINISTRATION – CMS
200 Independence Avenue, SW
Room 303-D
Washington, DC 20201
877-267-2323 (Voice - Toll-free)
202-690-6145 (Voice, Press Office)
202-690-7159 (FAX)
question@cms.gov
www.cms.gov

"As of July 1, 2001, the Health Care Financing Administration (HCFA) is now the Centers for Medicare & Medicaid Services (CMS). It's more than just a new name – it's an increased emphasis on responsiveness to beneficiaries and providers, and quality improvement." – *cms.gov*

AREA AGENCIES ON AGING
Eldercare Locator
927 15th St. NW, 6th Floor
Washington, DC 20005
202-296-8130
Eldercare Locator: 800-677-1116
www.n4a.org
www.eldercare.gov

"N4A's primary mission is to build the capacity of its members to help older persons and persons with disabilities live with dignity and choices in their homes and communities for as long as possible." – *n4a.org*

FIRST GOV FOR SENIORS
www.seniors.gov

"Accessed via a World-Wide-Web browser, the Internet has become an important communication vehicle for obtaining information about government services. Most Federal agencies now have websites. Because the web is not always customer-friendly, individuals seeking information about a particular agency's services may need to make an extensive search, i.e. "surf the net" to find the information they seek. Members of the public should be able to go to one comprehensive website to help them find the particular agency(ies) to satisfy their needs. FirstGov for Seniors was designed with those needs in mind. FirstGov for Seniors will empower citizens to obtain valuable health and security information and services at one location via the Internet".
– *FirstGov.org*

NATIONAL INSTITUTE ON AGING
www.nih.gov/nia

"The National Institute on Aging (NIA), one of the 25 institutes and centers of the National Institutes of Health, leads a broad scientific effort to understand the nature of aging and to extend the healthy, active years of life. In 1974, Congress granted authority to form the National Institute on Aging to provide leadership in aging research, training, health information dissemination, and other programs relevant to aging and older people. Subsequent amendments to this legislation designated the NIA as the primary federal agency on Alzheimer's disease research." – *nih.gov*

Missouri Guide for Seniors – Seventh Edition
MISSOURI DEPARTMENT OF HEALTH AND SENIOR SERVICES
Missouri Division of Senior Services
912 Wildwood Drive
P.O. Box 1337
Jefferson City, MO 65102
Phone: (573) 751-3082

Legal Resources

RUDY D. BECK, ATTORNEY AT LAW
Member: National Academy of Elder Law Attorneys
2777 West Clay St.
St. Charles, MO 63301
Phone: 636-946-7899

Rudy Beck is a trusted professional, who is an expert in Elder Law. Although Rudy practices law in the state of Missouri, he is happy to answer questions when he can. Please let him know that you found him through the Aging Answers publication. This is one example of a TRULY competent (and fantastic) Elder Law Attorney!

COMMISSION ON LEGAL PROBLEMS OF THE ELDERLY
www.abanet.org/elderly

"The mission of the ABA Commission on Law and Aging is to strengthen and secure the legal rights, dignity, autonomy, quality of life, and quality of care of elders. It carries out this mission through research, policy development, technical assistance, advocacy, education, and training." – *abanet.org*

NATIONAL ACADEMY OF ELDER LAW ATTORNEYS
1604 N Country Club Road
Tucson, AZ 85716 USA
www.naela.org

"The National Academy of Elder Law Attorneys, Inc. is a non-profit association that assists lawyers, bar organizations and others who work with older clients and their families. Established in 1987, the Academy provides a resource of information, education, networking and assistance to those who must deal with the many specialized issues involved with legal services to the elderly and disabled. The mission of the National Academy of Elder Law Attorneys is to establish NAELA members as the premier providers of legal advocacy, guidance, and services to enhance the lives of people as they age." – *naela.org*

SENIORLAW
www.seniorlaw.com

"This is a Web site where senior citizens, their families, attorneys, social workers, and financial planners, can access information about Elder Law, Medicare, Medicaid, estate planning, trusts and the rights of the elderly and disabled." – *seniorlaw.com*

Caregiver Resources: Home Care and Adult Day Care

NATIONAL ADULT DAY SERVICES ASSOCIATION, INC.
8201 Greensboro Drive, Suite 300
McLean, Virginia 22102
Toll Free Phone: (866) 890-7357 or (703) 610-9035
Fax: (703) 610-9005
E-mail: info@nadsa.org
www.nadsa.org

"The National Adult Day Services Association (NADSA) is the leading voice of the rapidly growing adult day service (ADS) industry in the United States, and the national focal point for adult day services providers. NADSA is a 20-year-old organization committed to providing its members with effective national advocacy, educational and networking opportunities, technical assistance, research and communication services." – *nadsa.org*

NATIONAL ASSOCIATION FOR HOME CARE
228 7th Street, SE
Washington, DC 20003
Phone: 202/547-7424
Fax: 202/547-3540
www.nahc.org

"NAHC believes that Americans should receive health care and social services in their own homes, so far as this is possible. Senior citizens and other vulnerable groups should be able to live in independence through the assistance of home care services, making institutionalization a last resort. NAHC seeks to reverse the current bias that places hundreds of thousands, possibly millions, of fragile children and chronically ill seniors in nursing homes or retained in hospitals when they could receive equal or better care at home. NAHC believes that home care keeps families together and is devoted to doing all in its power to preserve the sanctity of the American family, the bedrock of American democracy." – *nahc.org*

ABLEDATA – ASSISTIVE DEVICES
8630 Fenton Street, Suite 930
Silver Spring, MD 20910
Phone: 800/227-0216.
Fax: 301/608-8958.
TTY: 301/608-8912.
www.abledata.com

"ABLEDATA is a federally funded project whose primary mission is to provide information on assistive technology and rehabilitation equipment available from domestic and international sources to consumers, organizations, professionals, and caregivers within the United States. The ABLEDATA database contains information on more than 29,000 assistive technology products (over 19,000 of which are currently available), from white canes to voice output programs. The database contains detailed descriptions of each product including price and company information. The database also contains information on non-commercial prototypes, customized and one-of-a-kind products, and do-it-yourself designs. To select devices most appropriate to your needs, we suggest combining ABLEDATA information with professional advice, product evaluations, and hands-on product trials."
– *abledata.com*

MEALS ON WHEELS ASSOCIATION OF AMERICA
www.mealsonwheelsassn.org

"The Meals On Wheels Association of America represents those who provide congregate and home-delivered meal services to people in need. Our mission is to provide visionary leadership and professional training, and to develop partnerships that will ensure the provision of quality nutrition services."
– *mealsonwheelsassn.org*

ASSISTGUIDE INC.
2448 Centerline Industrial Drive
Maryland Heights, Missouri 63043
Phone: 877-703-1803
www.AssistGuide.com

"AssistGuide provides Senior and Disability Information and other Innovative Resources to the Senior and Disability Markets. We are the Interactive Community for Health Care Providers, Patients, Family Members, and Caregivers to find Senior and Disability Products, Services, and Support AssistGuide connects Providers, Employers, and State Governments online to enable Consumers to find the information and assistance they need today." – *assistguide.com*

Caregiver Resources: Hospice

PARTNERSHIP FOR CARING
1620 Eye Street NW, Suite 202,
Washington, DC 20006
Phone: 202-296-8071
Fax: 202-296-8352
Hotline: 800-989-9455
pfc@partnershipforcaring.org
www.partnershipforcaring.org

"Partnership for Caring: America's Voices for the Dying is a national, nonprofit organization devoted to raising consumer expectations for excellent end-of-life care and increasing demand for such care. It is the only end-of-life organization that partners individuals and organizations — consumers and professionals — in a powerful collaboration of voices. We raise our voices to demand that society improve how it cares for dying people and their loved ones." – *partnershipforcaring.org*

HOSPICE FOUNDATION OF AMERICA
2001 S St. NW #300
Washington DC 20009
phone: 1-800-854-3402
fax: (202) 638-5312
www.hospicefoundation.org

"Hospice Foundation of America is a not-for-profit organization that provides leadership in the development and application of hospice and its philosophy of care. Through programs of professional development, research, public education and information, Hospice Foundation of America assists those who cope either personally or professionally with terminal illness, death, and the process of grief." – *hospicefoundation.org*

NATIONAL HOSPICE & PALLIATIVE CARE ORGANIZATION (NHPCO)
1700 Diagonal Road, Suite 625
Alexandria, Virginia 22314
703/837-1500 (phone)
703/837-1233 (fax)
The NHPCO Helpline: 800-658-8898
www.nhpco.org

"The National Hospice and Palliative Care Organization (NHPCO) is the largest nonprofit membership organization representing hospice and palliative care programs and professionals in the United States. The organization is committed to improving end of life care and expanding access to hospice care with the goal of profoundly enhancing quality of life for people dying in America and their loved ones." – *nhpco.org*

Resources for Caregivers: Housing

THE ASSISTED LIVING FEDERATION OF AMERICA
11200 Waples Mill Rd
Suite 150
Fairfax, VA 22030
(t) 703.691.8100
(f) 703.691.8106
info@alfa.org
www.alfa.org

"The Assisted Living Federation of America (ALFA) represents over 7,000 for-profit and not-for-profit providers of assisted living, continuing care retirement communities, independent living and other forms of housing and services. Founded in 1990 to advance the assisted living industry and enhance the quality of life for the approximately one million consumers it serves, ALFA broadened its membership in 1999 to embrace the full range of housing and care providers who share ALFA's consumer-focused philosophy of care." – *alfa.org*

———————————————————

NATIONAL SHARED HOUSING RESOURCE CENTER
www.nationalsharedhousing.org

"For a growing number of Americans faced with losing their independence, shared housing is an affordable and viable alternative. A home sharer might be a senior citizen, a person with disabilities, a homeless person, a single parent, an AIDS patient, or simply a person wishing to share his or her life with others. For these people, shared housing offers companionship, security, mutual support and much more. Shared living has been known to enhance the health and well-being of all people and often prevents unnecessary and premature institutionalization. It also preserves neighborhoods and saves housing and healthcare dollars. Shared housing programs fall into one of two categories: Match-up programs, which help home providers find a compatible home seeker to pay rent or possibly provide services in exchange for a reduction in rent; and shared living residences, which involve a number of people living cooperatively as an unrelated family in a large dwelling." – *nationalsharedhousing.org*

NATIONAL CENTER FOR ASSISTED LIVING – NCAL
1201 L Street, NW
Washington, DC 20005
202-842-4444
www.ncal.org

"The National Center for Assisted Living (NCAL) is the assisted living voice of the American Health Care Association (AHCA), the nation's largest organization representing long-term care." – *ncal.org*

AMERICAN ASSOCIATION OF HOMES
AND SERVICES FOR THE AGING – AAHSA
2519 Connecticut Ave. NW
Washington, DC 20008
800-508-9442
www.aahsa.org

"The American Association of Homes and Services for the Aging (AAHSA) is committed to advancing the vision of healthy, affordable, ethical aging services for America. The association represents 5,600 mission-driven, not-for-profit nursing homes, continuing care retirement communities, assisted living and senior housing facilities, and home and community-based service providers. Every day, AAHSA's members serve one million older persons across the country. AAHSA has state association partners that represent AAHSA members in most states." – *aahsa.org*

The Eden Alternative™
www.edenalt.org

"The core concept of The Eden Alternative™ is strikingly simple. We must teach ourselves to see the environments as habitats for human beings rather than facilities for the frail and elderly. We must learn what Mother Nature has to teach us about the creation of vibrant, vigorous habitats. The Eden Alternative™ shows us how companion animals, the opportunity to give meaningful care to other living creatures, and the variety and spontaneity that mark an enlivened environment can succeed where pills and therapies fail. Our goal is to help people weave together the philosophy of The Eden Alternative™ with the real world of daily practice." – *edenalt.org*

Caregiver Resources: Geriatric Care Management

National Association of Professional Geriatric Care Managers
1604 N Country Club Road
Tucson, AZ 85716 USA
www.caremanager.org

"GCM is a non-profit, professional organization of practitioners whose goal is the advancement of dignified care for the elderly and their families. With more than 1,500 members, GCM is committed to maximizing the independence and autonomy of elders while striving to ensure that the highest quality and most cost-effective health and human services are used when and where appropriate." – *caremanager.org*

MID WEST CHAPTER – NAT'L ASSOC. OF PROFESSIONAL GERIATRIC CARE MANAGERS
www.midwestgcm.org

"Mid-West GCM is a non-profit, professional organization of practitioners whose goal is the advancement of dignified care for the elderly and their families. With more than 1,500 members nationally, GCM is committed to maximizing the independence and autonomy of elders while striving to ensure that the highest quality and most cost-effective health and human services are used when and where appropriate." – *midwestgcm.org*

SENIOR CARE SOLUTIONS, INC.
The Most Trusted Resource for Elder Care Consulting and Long-Term Care Insurance
1-877-529-0550
www.seniorcaresolutionsinc.com
www.seniorcaresolutionsltc.com
www.theltcexpert.com

"Senior Care Solutions, Inc. provides a vast array of services for families, aging adults and Long-Term Care Insurance consumers, as well as industry professionals.

As Long-Term Care Experts, we assist consumers, insurance agents, financial planners and other industry professionals by providing:

- Education on Long-Term Care Insurance Plans
- Information on the cost of Long-Term Care Insurance
- Detailed Plan Design Specific to Individual Needs
- Strategies on Financially Surviving the Cost of Long-Term Care
- Long-Term Care Seminars and Workshops
- Expert Speakers on Long-Term Care and LTC Insurance

As Elder Care Consultants and Geriatric Care Managers, Senior Care Solutions, Inc. provides expert assistance and guidance for aging adults at every level of care.

Our services are designed to assist families and seniors navigate the complicated health care system, and help them to make informed decisions about the type of care needed. Many families struggle to find assistance with the personal care needs for their family members, and are not sure if an aging adult should remain in their home, or transition to an alternative living situation. An older person may need assistance with home care, assisted living, nursing home care, or other social service needs such as grocery delivery, transportation to MD appointments, or bill paying."
– *seniorcaresolutionsinc.com*

Caregiver Resources: Medications

AMERICAN PHARMACEUTICAL ASSOCIATION – APhA
mail@aphanet.org
www.aphanet.org/
2215 Constitution Avenue, NW
Washington, DC 20037-2985
800-237-APHA (Voice - Toll-free)
202-628-4410 (Voice)
202-783-2351 (FAX)
www.aphanet.org

"The American Pharmacists Association (APhA), the national professional society of pharmacists, founded in 1852 as the American Pharmaceutical Association, is the first established and largest professional association of pharmacists in the United States. The more than 50,000 members of APhA include practicing pharmacists, pharmaceutical scientists, pharmacy students, pharmacy technicians, and others interested in advancing the profession. The Association is a leader in providing professional information and education for pharmacists and an advocate for improved health of the American public through the provision of comprehensive pharmaceutical care." – *aphanet.org*

─────────────────────────

CENTER WATCH – CLINICAL DRUG TRIALS
www.centerwatch.com

"We are a company dedicated to providing patients and their advocates with a variety of information services about clinical research. Our web site – *www.centerwatch.com* – provides an extensive list of IRB approved clinical trials being conducted internationally. Many of these trials may be appropriate for your participation. Our web site also lists promising therapies newly approved by the FDA (Food and Drug Administration)." – *centerwatch.com*

─────────────────────────

MEDLINEplus
www.nlm.nih.gov/medlineplus

"Health professionals and consumers alike can depend on it for information that is authoritative and up to date. MEDLINEplus has extensive information from the National Institutes of Health and other trusted sources on over 600 diseases and conditions. There are also lists of hospitals and physicians, a medical encyclopedia and a medical dictionary, health information in Spanish, extensive information on prescription and nonprescription drugs, health information from the media, and links to thousands of clinical trials. MEDLINEplus is updated daily and can be bookmarked at the URL: medlineplus.gov. There is no advertising on this site, nor does MEDLINEplus endorse any company or product." – *MEDLinePlus.gov*

─────────────────────────

Caregiver Resources: Finding Doctors

AMERICAN MEDICAL ASSOCIATION – AMA
amalibrary@ama-assn.org
515 North State Street
Chicago, IL 60610
800-621-8335 (Voice - Toll-free, For Physicians Only)
312-464-4818 (Voice)
www.ama-assn.org

"The AMA is the nation's leader in promoting professionalism in medicine and setting standards for medical education, practice, and ethics." – *ama-assn.org*

GERONTOLOGICAL SOCIETY OF AMERICA
www.geron.org

"The Gerontological Society of America is a non-profit professional organization with more than 5000 members in the field of aging. GSA provides researchers, educators, practitioners, and policy makers with opportunities to understand, advance, integrate, and use basic and applied research on aging to improve the quality of life as one ages." – *geron.org*

Caregiver Resources: Caregiver Organizations and Support

CENTER FOR FAMILY CAREGIVERS
PO BOX 224
Park Ridge, IL 60068
773-334-5794
www.familycaregivers.org

"Through The Center for Family Caregivers, we will help family members understand their caregiving journeys—the how's, why's and when's. Through our Kits for Caregivers program, family caregivers will learn how to cope throughout their caregiving experiences—when they first begin to care for an aging relative, to when they've been a caregiver for several years, to when their caregiving role ends." – *familycaregivers.org*

CHILDREN OF AGING PARENTS
1609 Woodbourne Road, Suite 302A
Levittown, PA 19057 USA
800-277-7294
www.caps4caregivers.org

"Children of Aging Parents is a nonprofit, charitable organization whose mission is to assist the nation's nearly 54 million caregivers of the elderly or chronically ill with reliable information, referrals and support, and to heighten public awareness that the health of the family caregivers is essential to ensure quality care of the nation's growing elderly population. Currently CAPS averages about 18,000 requests for assistance each year and the number is increasing. In 1995, there were 33 million Americans over the age of 65. In 2020, there will be almost 70 million, doubling in less than 25 years. Over 23 percent of all US households contain a caregiver. This translates into an estimated 22,411,200 caregiving households nationwide. The average caregiver is 46 years old. Seven in 10 caregivers (73 percent) are female. Only 5.5 percent of the over-65 population resides in nursing homes."
– *caps4caregivers.org*

NATIONAL FAMILY CAREGIVERS ASSOCIATION
10400 Connecticut Avenue, #500
Kensington, MD 20895-3944 USA
800-896-3650
www.nfcacares.org

"The National Family Caregivers Association (NFCA) exists to support family caregivers and to speak out publicly for caregivers' needs. NFCA espouses a philosophy of self-advocacy and self-care that is predicated on the belief that caregivers who choose to take charge of their lives, and see caregiving as but one of its facets, are in a position to be happier and healthier individuals. They are then able to have a higher quality of life and to make a more positive contribution to the well being of their care recipient, all of which has a positive impact on society and health care costs. Through its services in the areas of education and information, support and validation, public awareness and advocacy, NFCA strives to minimize the disparity between a caregiver's quality of life and that of mainstream Americans." – *nfcacares.org*

AMERICAN SELF-HELP GROUP CLEARINGHOUSE – ASHC
ashc@cybernex.net
Saint Clare's Health Services
25 Pocono Road
Denville, NJ 07834-2995
800-367-6274 (Voice - In-state only)
973-326-6789 (Voice)
www.selfhelpgroups.org

"This guide has been developed to act as your starting point for exploring real-life support groups and networks that are available throughout the world and in your community."
– *selfhelpgroups.org*

THE WELL SPOUSE FOUNDATION
63 West Main Street — Suite H
Freehold, NJ 07728
1-800-838-0879
www.wellspouse.org

"Well Spouse is a national, not for profit membership organization which gives support to wives, husbands, and partners of the chronically ill and/or disabled. Well Spouse support groups meet

monthly. Here, our members can share their thoughts and feelings openly with others facing similar circumstances in a supportive, non-judgmental environment. WS support groups are also an excellent source for information on a wide-range of practical issues facing spousal caregivers. Well Spouse support groups exist or are being formed in many areas of the country."
– *wellspouse.org*

Other Caregiver Sites of Interest:

www.caregiving.com

www.caregiver.com

www.carescout.com

http://griefnet.org

Senior Advocacy and Interest Groups

NATIONAL CONSUMERS LEAGUE
1701 K Street, NW, Suite 1200
Washington, DC 20006
202-835-3323
www.natlconsumersleague.org

"Our mission is to identify, protect, represent, and advance the economic and social interests of consumers and workers. The National Consumers League is a private, nonprofit advocacy group representing consumers on marketplace and workplace issues. We are the nation's oldest consumer organization."
– *natlconsumersleague.org*

FAMILIES USA
www.familiesusa.org

"Families USA is a national nonprofit, non-partisan organization dedicated to the achievement of high-quality, affordable health care for all Americans. Working at the national, state, and community levels, we have earned a national reputation as an effective voice for health care consumers for over 20 years"
– familiesusa.org

ELDERWEB
www.elderweb.com

"ElderWeb was created by Karen Stevenson Brown, a CPA and a consultant with over 19 years of experience in long-term care, finance, and technology. Over its eight years of existence, ElderWeb has grown to include thousands of reviewed links to long-term care information, a searchable database of organizations, and an expanding library of articles and reports, news, and events." *– Elderweb.com*

UNITED SENIORS HEALTH COUNCIL – USHC
409 3rd St., SW, Suite 200
Washington, DC 20024
202-479-6673
www.unitedseniorshealth.org

"NCOA is the nation's first association of organizations and professionals dedicated to promoting the dignity, self-determination, well being, and contributions of older persons. Founded in 1950, NCOA is a private, nonprofit association of some 3,500 organizations and individuals that includes senior centers, adult day service centers, area agencies on aging, employment services, congregate meal sites, faith congregations, health centers, and senior housing." *– unitedseniorshealth.org*

AMERICAN HEALTH CARE ASSOCIATION
1201 L Street, N.W., Washington, DC 20005
phone: (202) 842-4444 fax: (202) 842-3860
www.ahca.org

"The American Health Care Association (AHCA) is a non-profit federation of affiliated state health organizations, together representing nearly 12,000 non-profit and for-profit assisted living, nursing facility, developmentally-disabled, and subacute care providers that care for more than 1.5 million elderly and disabled individuals nationally." – *ahca.org*

———————————————————

ALLIANCE FOR RETIRED AMERICANS
888 16th St., N.W.
Suite 520
Washington, D.C. 20006
Phone: 888-373-6497
Fax: 202-974-8256
arawebadmin@retiredamericans.org
www.retiredamericans.org

"The mission of the Alliance for Retired Americans is to ensure social and economic justice and full civil rights for all citizens so that they may enjoy lives of dignity, personal and family fulfillment and security. The Alliance believes that all older and retired persons have a responsibility to strive to create a society which incorporates these goals and rights; and that retirement provides them with opportunities to pursue new and expanded activities with their unions, civic organizations, and their communities."
– *retiredamericans.org*

———————————————————

AMERICAN SOCIETY ON AGING – ASA
info@asaging.org
833 Market Street
Suite 511
San Francisco, CA 94103
415-974-9600 (Voice)
415-974-0300 (FAX)
www.asaging.org/

"ASA is a nonprofit organization committed to enhancing the knowledge and skills of those working with older adults and their families. Explore our publications and resources, utilize our educational programs and diversity initiatives, and share knowledge with the largest network of professionals in the field of aging." – *asaging.org*

ALLIANCE FOR AGING RESEARCH
info@agingresearch.org
2021 K Street, NW
Suite 305
Washington, DC 20006
800-639-2421 (Voice - Toll-free, Office)
202-293-2856 (Voice,)
202-785-8574 (FAX,)
www.agingresearch.org

"The private, not-for-profit Alliance for Aging Research is the nation's leading citizen advocacy organization for improving the health and independence of Americans as they age. The Alliance was founded in 1986 to promote medical and behavioral research into the aging process. Since then, and as the explosion of the Senior Boom approaches, the Alliance has become the voice for Baby Boomer health by developing, implementing and advocating programs in research, professional and consumer health education and public policy."– *agingresearch.org*

AARP
www.aarp.org

"With over 35 million members, AARP is the leading nonprofit, nonpartisan membership organization for people age 50 and over in the United States. The group is known for providing a host of services to this ever-growing segment of the population by:

- Informing members and the public on issues important to this age group
- Advocating on legislative, consumer and legal issues
- Promoting community service
- Offering a wide range of special products and services to members

Membership in AARP is open to any person age 50 or above. With 25 percent of the U.S. population in the 50+ category, nearly half of all people in this age bracket are AARP members. However, U.S. citizenship is not a requirement for membership; over 40,000 members live outside the United States. People also do not have to be retired to join. In fact, 44 percent of AARP members work part time or full time. For these reasons, AARP shortened its name in 1999 from the American Association of Retired Persons to just four letters: AARP. The median age of AARP members is 65, and slightly more than half of them are women." – *aarp.org*

BENEFITS CHECK-UP
http://www.benefitscheckup.org

"The BenefitsCheckUp is the nation's most comprehensive online service to screen for federal, state and some local private and public benefits for older adults (ages 55 and over). It contains over 1,100 different programs from all fifty states (including the District of Columbia). On average there are 50 to 70 programs available to individuals per state. In addition to identifying the programs that a person may be eligible to receive, BenefitsCheckUp also provides a detailed description of the programs, local contacts for additional information (typically the addresses and phone numbers of where to apply for the programs), and materials to help successfully apply for each program." – *benefitscheckup.org*

Miscellaneous Sites of Interest:

Mayo Clinic
www.mayohealth.org

On Health
www.my.webmd.com

Specific Disease Processes and Organizations On-Line:

National Alzheimer's Association
www.alz.org

Alzheimer's Research Forum
www.alzforum.org

Alzheimer's Disease Education and Referral
www.alzheimers.org

American Cancer Society
www.cancer.org

American Diabetes Association
www.diabetes.org

American Heart Association
www.americanheart.org

American Stroke Association
strokeassociation@heart.org
A Division of American Heart Association
7272 Greenville Avenue
Dallas, TX 75231
888-4STROKE (Voice - Toll-free)
www.strokeassociation.org

Arthritis Foundation
www.arthritis.org

National Organization for Rare Disorders
www.rarediseases.org

National Association for Continence
www.nafc.org

NATIONAL OSTEOPOROSIS FOUNDATION
www.nof.org

NATIONAL SLEEP FOUNDATION
www.sleepfoundation.org

PARKINSON'S RESOURCE ORGANIZATION
www.parkinsonsresource.org

SELF HELP FOR HARD OF HEARING PEOPLE
www.shhh.org

LIGHTHOUSE NATIONAL CENTER FOR VISION AND AGING – NCVA
info@lighthouse.org
111 East 59th Street
New York, NY 10022
800-829-0500 (Voice - Toll-free, Information and Resource Serv.)
212-821-9200 (Voice)
212-821-9784 (FAX)
212-821-9713 (Voice - TDD)
www.lighthouse.org/

About the Author

Valerie VanBooven is a *Registered Nurse* and *Certified Care Manager*, as well as a licensed *Life and Health Agent* in Missouri. After several years of discharge planning and case management for the Unity Health System in St. Louis, Valerie incorporated her own business.

In 1999, *Senior Care Solutions, Inc.* was formed. Now, Valerie is a dedicated Geriatric Care Manager and Long-Term Care Expert.

"I have seen so many families struggle to pay for long-term care costs out of pocket. This can be a devastating situation for everyone involved. My goal is to provide education regarding Long-Term Care Insurance, and to help families protect what they have worked so hard to accumulate. I have seen many other families use their Long-Term Care Insurance benefits when they needed them, and the bottom line is, it works!"

Valerie is the National Long-Term Care Expert for *AssistGuide.com*, which includes monthly chats for caregivers, and a monthly column titled *"Ask Valerie"*, regarding elder care needs. Valerie is the author of *"Long-Term Care Planning for Insurance Professionals"* published in May 2002 (National Business Institute), and *"Nursing Home Malpractice: From Investigation to Trial"*, April 2003 (National Business Institute). She also authors a monthly column for *Progressive Woman Magazine*, titled "Your Elder Care Resource".

Mid 2002, Valerie was selected as one of 16 presenters to embark on a Nationwide Tour providing educational seminars for Federal Employees on the new Federal Long-Term Care Insurance Program. Valerie is now a regular visitor to the State Department, various bases and forts throughout the country, and various Federal Buildings. She had presented to thousands of attendees, in over 180 presentations in as little as 5 months.

Valerie is a regular guest speaker for many organizations and groups throughout the country, on various topics related to the aging process, caregiving, long-term care issues, and long-term care insurance. She is a member of the National Speakers Association, The National Association of Professional Geriatric Care Managers, Midwest Geriatric Care Managers, and the St. Louis Regional Commerce and Growth Association. She has been a featured guest on various talk radio programs such as The Dave Glover Show, St. Louis On The Air with Greg Freeman, MoneyTalk with Bob HardCastle, Coping with Caregiving with Jacqueline Marcell, and Vital Signs with Dr. Randy Tobler.

Valerie's websites include:

www.seniorcaresolutionsinc.com

www.theltcexpert.com

www.seniorcaresolutionsltc.com

www.aginganswer.com

Valerie's email address:

Valerie@seniorcaresolutionsinc.com